Barbara Howard Lundegaard

September 1993

✠ Minneapolis ✠

Child Development

D1451660

"*The Picture of Health* will help you get in touch with your true self. The Bible reveals that God speaks to us in dreams and symbols. Lucia helps us hear and see what this inner truth is telling us. Her book and its exercises starts us on a path of self-discovery and healing."

—Bernie Siegel

THE PICTURE OF HEALTH

Other Books by Lucia Capacchione:

The Power of Your Other Hand
The Creative Journal: The Art of Finding Yourself
The Well-Being Journal: Drawing on Your Inner Power to Heal Yourself
The Creative Journal for Children: A Guide for Parents, Teachers, and Counselors
The Creative Journal: A Handbook for Teens
Lighten Up Your Body, Lighten Up Your Life, co-authored with Elizabeth Johnson and James Strohecker

Audiotape

Well-Being Journal Meditations

For information regarding Lucia Capacchione's books, lectures, workshops, and trainings, contact:

INNERWORKS
1341 Ocean Ave. #100
Santa Monica, CA 90401
(213) 285-9489

THE PICTURE OF HEALTH

Healing Your Life With Art

Lucia Capacchione

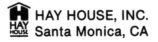

HAY HOUSE, INC.
Santa Monica, CA

THE PICTURE OF HEALTH
Healing Your Life With Art
by Lucia Capacchione

The author of this book does not dispense medical advice nor prescribe
the use of any technique as a form of treatment for physical or medical
problems without the advice of a physician, either directly or indirectly. The
intent of the author is only to offer information of a general nature to help
you in your quest for physical fitness and good health. In the event you use
any of the information in this book for yourself, the author and the
publisher assume no responsibility for your actions.

Library of Congress Catalog Card No. 89-80790

Library of Congress Cataloging-in-Publication Data

Capacchione, Lucia
     The picture of health : healing your life through art / Lucia
Capacchione.
        p.   cm.
     Includes bibliographical references.
     ISBN: 0-937611-68-9 : $12.00
     1. Art therapy.   I. Title
RC489.A7C37   1990
615.8'5156—dc20   89-80790
                                                                CIP

ISBN: 0-937611-68-9

Typesetting: Freedmen's Organization, Los Angeles, CA
Printed and Bound in the United States of America by
Delta Lithograph Co. of Valencia, CA

90 91 92 93 94 95   10 9 8 7 6 5 4 3 2 1
First Printing, March 1990

Published and distributed in the United States by
Hay House, Inc.
501 Santa Monica Boulevard
Post Office Box 2212
Santa Monica, California   90406   USA

Printed in the United States of America

Dedicated with love and gratitude
to
the healing power of creativity
which dwells
in every human heart.

THANKS

To the contributors:
Kathy Baptista
Donna Jean Barna
Kathleen Bevacqua
Matthew Bond
Eve Eschner
Ben Hedges
David Jarvis
Ken Johnston
Pamela Karle
Sue Maxwell
Carole Melody
Jane Murphy
Dan Olmos
Sondra Phillips
Val Taylor
Christina Wilson

To all the students and clients who helped field-test the material in this book.

To the Center for the Healing Arts, where I participated in their pioneering work with the arts as a healing modality, and led support groups for people with life-threatening diseases.

To the L.A. Center for Living where I field-tested much of the material in this book in my workshops for persons with AIDS and other life-threatening and chronic diseases.

To Elizabeth Lord and Heather Williams for their support and input.

To James Strohecker and Nancy Shaw Strohecker, my creative associates, for their expertise and invaluable support in seeing this project through all its phases—from concept development and research to editing and word processing.

To my editors at Hay House, Linda Laucella, Valerie Marz, Kathy Garrett, and Andrew Ettinger for their confidence, encouragement, and enthusiasm.

To the staff at Hay House, to its President, Linda Tomchin, and its Vice President, Jim Leary, for their support and faith in my work.

And to Louise Hay for inspiring me over the years through her own work and shining example.

Contents

Preface

Dear Reader:

This book is about healing with art. It offers you a new way to look at yourself and to create a healthy life. Through scribbling, drawing, and collage you will learn to "think and feel" on paper. Then you will be shown how to decode the messages contained in your spontaneous art and translate your insights through the written word. You will also learn to reshape your life from the inside out through visual affirmations—pictures and words of how you want to experience your life. No special talent or training in art is required to do these activities. All you need is the willingness to express your own truth, and the desire to love and heal yourself.

These techniques have been used successfully in dealing with a full range of human issues: physical illness, relationship conflicts, divorce, death of a loved one, career crisis, creative blocks, and "failures." Since the mid-1970s I have shared my discoveries at seminars for people of all ages and occupations: in schools and colleges, churches, corporations, counseling centers, and spiritual retreats. Over the years I have documented my discoveries and techniques in several books. The feedback has been so inspiring, especially in regard to the healing power of art, that I was moved to write this book. It includes not only my personal story and triumph over difficult odds and a life-threatening condition, but the impressive success stories of others.

I became an art therapist in 1975 after healing an "incurable" disease primarily through spontaneous drawing and writing. At the time of my illness, I was a professional artist and teacher. I had never heard of art therapy, and there were no popular books on the subject. My spontaneous self-exploration through art was undoubtedly guided by a higher healing power within, taking me step by step back home to my Inner Self.

When you read my story you will see how the Inner Artist has played the role of healer throughout my life. Through the writing and drawing exercises, affirmations, visualizations, meditations, and inspirational stories, I hope you find the healing power of *your own* Inner Artist. I have found that tremendous love—for yourself and for others—becomes the overflowing pot of gold at the end of the rainbow. It comes with the joy of finding and expressing your own truth.

Lucia Capacchione
Santa Monica, California

Introduction

At the bottom of the abyss comes the voice of salvation. The black moment is the moment when the real message is going to come. At the darkest moment comes the light.
—Joseph Campbell
The Power of Myth

My life is a continuing lesson in creativity and healing. I discovered the healing power of picture making at an early age. At nine years old I suffered a long bout of bronchial pneumonia: high fevers, headaches, and breathing difficulties. At times the fever was so high I hallucinated deep echoing voices rumbling incoherently in my head. They seemed to be coming from the bowels of the earth, and I thought of them as "sound monsters." I also had visual hallucinations: garish, neon-colored figures dancing on the walls. Terrified, I tried to describe what I had seen and heard to my parents and to the doctor, who made house calls in those days. They tried to reassure me that I was "just hallucinating" because of the fever, but I didn't understand such a big word. They seemed to be saying that it was all in my head, but that was no comfort. It *felt* real and I was scared.

When I was well enough to sit up, my mother gave me a very special surprise, a sky-blue bed tray with pink flower decals on its surface. The tray had four legs and could be adjusted to slant like a drafting table. Then the mother of one of my playmates came to visit, and gave me a wonderful book on how to draw. It was filled with pictures and diagrams of how to draw people, trees, animals, and cartoons. The bed tray became an easel and I spent my days drawing and copying the pictures in the book.

In a sense, I drew myself back to health. At the same time, a new world opened up and my life was changed forever. Drawing put me into such a joyful state, I never wanted to stop. After so much time lying helplessly in bed, overwhelmed by illness and secretly wondering what was happening to me, I was now able to do something, to make something that pleased me.

Family and friends who visited me during my convalescence and saw my drawings said that I had "talent" and "artistic ability." The discovery that I could draw was like falling heir to a completely unexpected inheritance. I endured the next few years in parochial school by drawing at every opportunity. I survived three Catholic girls' high schools by sketching and painting and reading every art book I could find. But because of the common prejudice that you can't make a living at art, I did not seriously consider becoming an artist during those years.

However, at seventeen, something happened that changed the course of my life. Just before graduation from Immaculate Heart High School, I contracted a serious case of measles, followed by a relapse into bronchitis. It was a nightmare—as awful as the pneumonia I'd had at age nine, including the high fever and feelings of total helplessness. My only good memories were of the recovery period, sitting with that little bed tray doing watercolor landscapes from my imagination. Through the magic of my mind, I had vicariously experienced green poplar trees in spring spattered with golden specks of sunlight. I had created pale yellow beaches with cobalt blue seas where I ran on the sand and splashed in the surf. As I had fashioned my own beautiful world on paper, my body had begun to heal.

It was at that point that I decided to major in art in college, despite my father's admonitions that artists can't make a living. My response: "But it's what I love to do more than anything in the world." I knew that I had to follow my heart. I have never regretted my decision.

I was fortunate enough to find one of the most unique and innovative art departments in the country in my own backyard. In the late 1950s, the art department of Immaculate Heart College in Hollywood boasted a rare and prolific talent, Sister Mary Corita, resident artist and instructor. Although I was certain I had had enough of Catholic girls' schools, I could not resist the art department or its famous, diminutive "star."

Four years later, after receiving my B.A., I realized a dream I'd had since freshman year—to work for world-renowned designer Charles Eames at his studio in Venice, California. Although best known for the award-winning, revolutionary fiberglass and molded-plywood chairs bearing his name, he was also a fine photographer, filmmaker, and exhibit designer. The Eames office was truly a magical place. I felt like Alice in Wonderland—or like Josh in his Manhattan loft in the movie *Big*.

It was three years later that I learned once again the healing power of visual images and creative expression. By this time I had married a fellow designer, and we were living in a semirural area far from the city, friends, and familiar places. I felt very isolated while recovering from the difficult delivery of our first child. I can remember being overwhelmed with postpartum depression as I stood at the clothesline in the field behind our little country cottage. The diapers hanging on the line seemed to stretch out into infinity. My college education and exciting career in design had never prepared me for this. Talk about the "blues"! I was asking myself, "What's wrong with this picture?"

Once again I turned inward and realized I still had the power to create. It had always pulled me out of difficult times before, and it would pull me out again. So during the baby's naps, I started doing artwork. At the kitchen table, next to piles of clean diapers and rows of baby bottles, I designed and printed greeting cards. In no time my creative juices were flowing and the depression lifted. The cards were accepted by shops and mail order companies, and I launched a part-time career as a freelance artist. Motherhood became a great adventure instead of an overwhelming burden, and a year later we had our second child.

Within a couple of years I was ready to take the next step and develop a line of serigraphs for exhibition. I had never shown my work in galleries before, so I was somewhat apprehensive. The business side of gallery art was a mystery to me, and I faced what all artists have to face: the possibility of rejection.

I'll never forget the morning I drove to East Los Angeles to buy paper for printing my serigraphs. It was November 22, 1963. En route to the paper supplier, I heard that President Kennedy had been shot in a motorcade in Texas. Like all the world, I was stunned. Shortly afterward I heard Walter Cronkite's voice coming from a nearby television set, announcing that the president was dead.

Once again I turned to art to try to make sense out of mystery and chaos. I dedicated the next year of my life to creating a series of posters illuminating inspirational words from my favorite poets and philosophers.

Quotes from Ranier Maria Rilke, Maria Montessori, R. Buckminster Fuller, Juan Ramon Jimenez, Kenneth Patchen, and Teilhard de Chardin floated through images of flowers and trees, birds and butterflies, meadows and mountains. I pictured a world of hope and love in contrast to the grim violence I saw in the media. My work was exhibited nationally and was eventually mass-produced for the poster market which was booming in the psychedelic late 1960s.

Later, I trained in the Montessori method of early education and became a successful child-development supervisor and then a toy designer. As a wife, mother, and busy professional woman, I led an extremely active life. But there was no time for the inner life, for introspection, or for listening to my deeper thoughts and feelings. Then one day life collapsed all around me like a house of cards. My parents' marriage faltered after thirty-five years, and my own marriage and business partnership ended overnight. I had been so focused on worldly success that I had not seen the warning signs. I had no idea what hit me. It was worse than any earthquake I had ever known while growing up in Los Angeles, and it shook me to my foundations. My entire world fell apart.

Upon filing for a divorce, I came down with mononucleosis. When I was well enough to function again, I left the design corporation that I had recently formed with my husband. I had to start my career and life all over again. There were four moves in two years and several freelance jobs as a designer and early education consultant. And of course, there was the big adjustment to life as a single parent. Thank God for my professional skills and my sheer determination to survive. But after three and a half years of constant change, with no time to catch my breath between crises, my body finally gave out.

I came down with a debilitating condition which remained undiagnosed at the time. Tests confirmed that it was not a recurrence of mononucleosis. Years later I learned it was a collagen disease for which there is no known cure. Collagen is the connective tissue in the body, the "glue" which holds us together. I had "come apart at the seams." I had come unglued. With uncanny precision, my body reflected my psychological state. The disease was the perfect metaphor for my life.

While I was ill, exhausted and unable to function, the doctors could not agree on what my condition was or what had caused it. Each specialist looked at the part he was trained to see, each prescribed a different medication, and all the medications caused side effects. Emotionally, this made my earlier bouts of pneumonia and measles seem like the common cold. This time I really feared for my life. I had lost all confidence in doctors, and knew with an instinctive certainty that continuing to take their medications would kill me.

So I turned to art once again, but this time I went inside and began drawing and writing my innermost feelings in a little blank book. Just expressing my feelings in the moment was liberating in itself. The fear, anger, and grief that had been buried so long all came out on paper. Later I drew and wrote about my life as I wanted it to be. Then by sharing my writings and drawings with a couple of close friends, I made an amazing discovery. I was not alone. My friends were really there for me, encouraging me to listen to myself, to be true to my own inner voices.

When I threw my medications away, and decided to change the course of treatment, my friends stood solidly behind me. They referred me to competent and compassionate health care professionals: a therapist, an acupressurist, and a medical doctor who practiced preventive medicine. During this time I continually drew and wrote in my personal journal. In spontaneous drawings, poetry, and reflective writing, I documented my inner healing journey. At times it appeared as a "dark night of the soul." For me it was certainly an initiation into the mysteries of healing the body and the mind.

After my full recovery, I returned to graduate school and then gave birth to a new career as an art therapist. Integrating journal keeping into my professional work, I was able to validate and expand the techniques which my Inner Artist and Inner Healer revealed to me during my illness. By teaching my clients to draw their feelings, wishes, and dreams in journals, I was able to help them become more responsible for dealing with every-day problems as they occurred.

I also discovered Jungian psychology, western metaphysics, and ancient spiritual traditions from the East which taught the power of the mind to create our own personal reality. My understanding of illness and healing deepened when I discovered Carl Jung's theory of the "wounded healer." He believed that one who has courageously survived an inner journey of facing disease and death can return empowered to help others in their healing process.

As an artist I had always known that I had the power to create magical worlds in my imagination and then translate the images into the outer world through the medium of ink, paint, and paper. But until my recovery from the collagen disease in 1973, I had never seen the direct connection between art and healing. It was at that time that I discovered how the creative process could be applied to healing and transforming one's life.

Treasure the chaos out of which order emerges.
Cherish the puzzlement leading to the light.
Deep inside this nest is the Self to be found.
                                        —My personal journal

In a Dark Time, the Eye Begins to See.
                                        —Theodore Roethke

1

Health: The Rapture of Being Alive

I think that what we're seeking is an experience of being alive, so that our life experiences on the purely physical plane will have resonances within our innermost being and reality, so that we actually feel the rapture of being alive.

—Joseph Campbell
The Power of Myth

Through the years I have come to a new understanding of the meaning of health. For me, health is wholeness—the experience of being fully alive. It is more than the absence of pain and disease. Health is an ongoing process—a dynamic interplay between the physical, emotional, mental, and spiritual aspects of one's being. It involves far more than a narrow focus on body, emotions, or thoughts. Being healthy is not just "eating right," exercising, reducing stress, or looking youthful. Every choice one makes and every element of one's lifestyle affects health: activities, relationships, home environment, and work.

I wrote this book in order to share the methods I have discovered for experiencing wholeness, health, and aliveness. These methods involve "healing from the inside out" through creative expression. They also invite you to love and understand your whole self—body, mind, and spirit.

Healing is an ongoing process. It isn't something that happens just once and then you are cured or healed forever. In fact, the terms *cured* and *healed* can be dangerous in the past tense, because they lead us to believe that there is a beginning, middle, and an end to the healing process. In

1

this approach the goal is to get "fixed" and then dismiss the problem. But true healing, on the contrary, is a moment-to-moment process of balancing oneself. It is just like breathing. It goes on as long as you are alive. Healing is also a process that *you* participate in. *It isn't something done to you.* Healing is an inside job.

When our vitality is blocked, we are in need of healing. These blocks often manifest themselves as physical pain and low energy. The body is a remarkable mirror, reflecting aspects of ourselves that we have ignored. For instance, I used to suffer from recurring lower back pain. Physiologically, the lower back *supports* the upper torso and allows us to be upright and move forward. At those times of back pain, through drawing and writing I discovered that I needed more support in my life. I was trying to do everything myself without asking others for help. I was also afraid that my new career as a writer would not support me financially. By discovering the psychological roots of my physical pain, I was able to recognize the attitudes and feelings I was holding in my back. As I changed my beliefs, the pain dissolved.

WHERE ARE WE GOING?

This book is about listening to your inner wisdom and creating a healthy life. We do this by drawing and coloring, collage and mirror work, visualization, writing, and affirmations. For clarification and inspiration I have included case studies and artwork from students and clients who have used my methods with great success. I have field-tested these activities with thousands of individuals in my workshops, classes, and private art therapy sessions.

My goal is to help you:
1. Find the mental/emotional roots of stress, pain, and disease.
2. Change negative limiting beliefs.
3. Discover the therapeutic power of creative expression.
4. Use the healing power of visual imagery.
5. Choose and create a healthy lifestyle.

A PICTURE IS WORTH A THOUSAND WORDS

"A picture is worth a thousand words." How many times have you heard this aphorism? It says a lot about the power of the visual image to convey meaning. We know from early cave paintings that graphic symbols and picture making preceded written language in cultural evolution. As Carl Jung pointed out, visual images and symbols are the language of the collective unconscious. They transcend culture and speak to our common human experience. When we sleep we dream in pictures, and when we are awake we fantasize and daydream in pictures. We remember in pictures, and we create and invent in pictures. We can also use pictures to heal ourselves and create a healthy lifestyle.

Art is a universal language. I have observed this firsthand as an educator and art therapist working with people from diverse cultures. While doing research on art as emotional expression, I asked groups to draw certain feelings such as anger, sadness, joy, fear, confusion, excitement, and peace. Regardless of sex or ethnic background, students used similar lines and colors to represent the same emotions. For example, the emotion *anger* was often scribbled in strong strokes of red or black.

As an art therapist I have observed that most people have lost their innate ability to make art. Artists have been elevated to a special place and separated from the rest of our society. It is said that artists are "different," "talented," or "creative."

The fact is, *we all have the ability to tap our inner resources and make meaningful pictures that can help heal our bodies, minds, and spirits, and enhance our lives.*

Marian's is a classic case. She came to me for counseling several months after being released from a drug and alcohol treatment center. She was participating in two 12-step programs, Alcoholics Anonymous and Narcotics Anonymous. However, she was living at home with her mother, in the same dysfunctional situation that contributed to her obsessive-compulsive behavior in the first place.

In an art therapy session, I asked Marian to draw a picture of herself and her family. She drew two screaming faces—one very large and one very small. As soon as she completed the drawing, she exclaimed: "Oh, my God! That's me and my mother fighting. I've *got* to get out of that house! I've got to move. If I stay there, I'll end up on drugs and booze again."

A few weeks later she did get her own apartment, and she gradually created a healthy life on her own. She told me later that she had to put that picture up on her wall. Whenever her resolve to live on her own wavered, she would sit and look at the picture. She said, "The message was so clear, it always motivated me to go house-hunting. Without that visual reminder, I probably would have fallen back into safety and dependence, and would have continued living with my mother. I hate to think what would have happened if I'd stayed there in the womb."

THE INNER ARTIST AS HEALER

For a number of years I have led workshops entitled "Finding the Healer Within." Many of the people who attend are struggling with life-threatening diseases or chronic pain. Others are dealing with life crises: career change, divorce, and the death of a loved one. When I introduce drawing activities, the most common reaction is: "I can't draw. I don't have any talent."

If that is your response too, then please relax. You are in for a big surprise. In this book, you will be guided to change this limiting belief. Make no mistake about it. This is just a belief. And like all beliefs, it can be replaced with a new one that serves you.

Now remember, I am not trying to turn you into a professional artist. The fact is that if you can put pen to paper and doodle or scribble, you *can* draw. In fact, when you doodle and scribble you *are* drawing, as you will discover later. It is your critical mind that jumps in and destroys any attempt to express yourself in lines and colors on paper. In childhood you may have been repeatedly told, "You can't draw," or something to that effect, and you believed it. So you avoided drawing and perhaps any artistic expression. Who wants to risk looking foolish and making art that is judged "stupid" or "ugly"?

As you do the activities in this book, there will be no critiques from the outside. The only judge you have to face is the one that sits in your mind.

As you set those critical and negative beliefs aside, you will regain your innate ability to express yourself through art. After drawing yourself and your world as they appear now, you will create the image of your life as you *want* it to be. Through the creative window of your imagination, you will see beyond your fears and limitations to a place where a more vital and fulfilling life awaits you.

The following drawing illustrates this point beautifully. It was done by Christina, who attended one of my workshops. For many years she had been grieving the loss of her sister, with whom she was very close. In this powerful drawing she was able to catch a glimpse of the "beauty" that lies beyond her own pain.

The written description that accompanies Christina's artwork demonstrates the profound psychological insight she gained from drawing her feelings out. She saw that in order to get to the beauty, she had to deal with her pain.

i see that i am on this side of the pain inside me and that the darkness and pain are the barriers. i see the hole and the beauty beyond the whole. i want to go thru it and see what else is there but in doing that i see i may also move beyond my own pain — get through it to the outside of me.

june 2, 1989

However, Christina had no idea how to do deal with her pain at that time. It seemed like an insurmountable task. But after faithfully doing journal writing and drawing for about three months, Christina was strong enough to picture both the beautiful landscape glimpsed in her first drawing as well as the darkness of her pain. This was a major breakthrough.

In the following drawing, which is a reversal of the first, she found a frightened, vulnerable, brokenhearted child named Tina who was hiding in the blackness and waiting for Christina to find her. Little Tina wants to put her leg out and step into the beautiful world that Christina has envisioned, but she is scared. At this time, Christina had been a graphic designer in the clutches of an immobilizing creative block. Doing this personal work in her journal removed the block and has given her a tool for dealing with it whenever her fear prevents creative expression in her work.

aug. 21, 1989

THE HEALING POWER OF IMAGERY

Imagination is the beginning of creation: You imagine what you desire; you will what you imagine; and at last you create what you will.

—George Bernard Shaw

Many people in my workshops ask, "What exactly is imagery?" Dr. Martin Rossman, a physician who has successfully used this technique in his private practice for the past 15 years, defines imagery in his critically acclaimed book, *Healing Yourself*:

> *Imagery is a flow of thoughts you can see, hear, feel, smell, or taste. An image is an inner representation of your experience or your fantasies—a way your mind codes, stores, and expresses information. Imagery is the currency of dreams and daydreams; memories and reminiscence; plans, projections, and possibilities. It is the language of the arts, the emotions, and most important, of the deeper self.*

In recent years scientists and medical doctors such as Carl O. Simonton, Stephanie Matthews-Simonton, Jean Achterberg, and Martin Rossman have demonstrated that imagery has a profound effect on the body and immune system. It appears that mental imagery can actually trigger the body's self-healing abilities.

Everyone can create imagery; it is an innate human ability. However, many of my students have told me that they couldn't use imagery because they couldn't see mental pictures. Imagery draws from *all* the senses, not just sight. (I call seeing mental pictures *visualization*.) In my workshops I usually demonstrate the use of imagery by asking people to describe in detail their last meal—the setting, tastes, smells, sounds, and colors. People are always able to do this with ease because they are free to choose their own perceptual mode. Some people think visually and tend to "see" experiences in their mind's eye. Auditory people rely on what they hear: ambient sound, speech, and music. Kinesthetic people rely on physically sensing the movement, texture, and feel of things. Although everyone generally uses all sensory modes, we each tend to favor one mode over the others. Some people will start by describing sounds, like bacon sizzling on the grill, others the smell of bread burning in the toaster, and still others will describe the sight of two bright yellow eggs sunny-side up. At this point I tell them, "What you just did is imagery."

Then I ask the group to describe an *imaginary* meal. Again they do this with relative ease, using all of their sense perceptions. I again point out to them that what they just did was mental imagery.

You may want to try this yourself right now, in the following brief imagery exercise.

IMAGERY EXERCISE

Close your eyes and allow yourself to re-experience the last meal you ate.

Where were you? Who were you with? What were you eating? What did you smell? How did it taste? What sounds did you hear? What did you see? What are the different textures you experienced? How did you feel after eating the meal?

Now imagine a meal you would love to have in the future. Money is no object; you can have this meal wherever you wish and have whatever you want. Close your eyes and allow your dream meal to happen in your imagination.

Where are you? Who are you with? What are you eating? How does it smell? How does it taste? What textures do you feel? What do you see? How do you feel as you eat this meal?

The fact is that you are using imagery all the time. You use imagery from past experiences, both pleasant and unpleasant, to guide your life. For instance, in choosing a restaurant, you sort through images of past experiences and match them with your present mood and taste. You consider the ambience, the odors and tastes of the food, the price range, location, and so forth. In just this way you can also use imagery to design a better, healthier life for yourself.

First, we use imagery to examine what is *not* working in our lives. Then we use imagery to help create what we want. Dr. Martin Rossman put it this way in *Healing Yourself:*

> *Imagery is a window on your inner world; a way of viewing your own ideas, feelings, and interpretations. But it is more than a mere window—it is a means of transformation and liberation from distortions in this realm that may unconsciously direct your life and shape your health.*

In this book you will learn to listen to the "hidden language of the body"—images, symbols, and metaphors—and apply the messages you receive to your everyday life. You will learn to use mental imagery as well as graphic imagery on paper. You will be "drawing your inner world out," making your invisible dreams and wishes visible.

For those of you who have difficulty creating visual images in the mind's eye, the art process will be helpful. After drawing pictures of your life the way you want it to be, you will take these graphic images into the mind through your eyes. In this way you are using many levels of experience and perception: imagination, sensory awareness, and memory. For you will now be able to mentally *recall* the visual impression you saw with your eyes. This is the same principle that is used in written affirmations. You read your positive affirmations, speak them, and memorize them so that they become part of your mental "bank account."

In drawing positive images on paper and reinforcing them through the sense of sight and memory, you are creating "visual affirmations." Designers and artists do this all the time. They make rough sketches of new ideas. They want to see with their physical eyes what is in their mind's eye. Why? Because they eventually want their ideas to take physical form. Whether it is the idea for a building, a mural, or a dress, the sketch is the first step. After that, the idea can be translated into scale models or mock-ups so that the artist can understand how the idea will look and function in three dimensions. From there, the blueprints or patterns can be developed so that the "idea" can be built or manufactured in final, life-size form. But it all starts with a simple sketch on paper.

WRITING YOUR WAY TO HEALTH

As a journalkeeper, I can attest to the healing power of writing out one's feelings. Writing has helped me release tension again and again by allowing me to face myself on the written page, to vent anger, give a voice to fear, and express confusion and doubt. In recent years, there has been scientific research corroborating what we journalkeepers have experienced firsthand.

Psychologist James W. Pennebaker found that writing down one's feelings about an illness or traumatic event actually contributes to improved efficiency of the immune system. The research involved a control-group study at Southern Methodist University in Dallas. Blood samples were taken before and after the writing experiment and again six weeks later. Dr. Pennebaker found that those who wrote about difficult experiences showed an increase in lymphocyte response, which indicates an enhanced ability to fight infection. The group who wrote about trivia showed no such strengthening of the immune system. Furthermore, the group who wrote about traumatic experiences made far fewer visits to the doctor in the six-month period following the experiment.

THE HEALING POWER OF YOUR OTHER HAND

I have discovered that writing with the nondominant hand taps directly into functions normally associated with the right hemisphere of the brain: intuition and emotional expression. As we know from recent brain research, the right hemisphere of the brain seems to specialize in non-verbal, visual-spatial functions. It is generally accepted, for instance, that drawing and other visual arts rely greatly upon right-brain processes. The same is true for mental imagery.

The left hemisphere of the brain processes verbal, mathematical, and logical information. It governs the ability to follow rules of grammar, spelling, and syntax, and makes it possible for people to use a common language for communicating. There are centers in the left hemisphere which, if damaged through disease or injury, will cause impairment of speech and language functions. Our school systems and our society as a whole emphasize and rely heavily on verbal and logical processes (the three R's), and we have been described as a "left-brained" culture. Certainly the arts, which develop right-brain skills, are the most neglected aspects of the curriculum in most schools.

The right brain controls the entire left side of the body, while the left brain controls the right side of the body. Interestingly enough, most people write with their right hand; the right hand is governed by the left (logical, verbal) side of the brain. However, some people who write with their right hands are actually "switch-overs." They were originally left-handed or ambidextrous individuals who were forced by parents or teachers to be like everybody else and write with the right, "correct" hand.

According to my research, no matter which hand you normally use for writing, when you write with your *other hand* you can access parts of your personality that are usually silent. Some of these parts or subpersonalities are the Inner Child, the Artist/Poet Within, the Inner Guide, and the Inner Healer.

The Inner Child is the emotional self that is sensitive and feels deeply. It is also spontaneous, playful, and extremely creative.

The Artist/Poet Within loves beauty and finds magic in the most ordinary experiences. This part of us also sees beyond appearance and can make the invisible visible through creative expression.

The Inner Guide comes from a deep reservoir of wisdom that we carry within. When tapped, it can help us resolve our problems and answer the questions we ask about our own life.

The Inner Healer is the power that we have to heal ourselves from within. As Hippocrates taught, "The natural healing force within each one of us is the greatest force in getting well."

The development of these subpersonalities is generally discouraged in our society. They all have in common a high sensitivity to feeling and intuition. This is where the "other hand" comes in. Emotional expression and intuitive wisdom can flow through the *other hand* with ease, simplicity, and the straightforward ring of truth. The analytical mind can step aside for a moment and give the emotional/intuitive mind a chance to express itself. The advantage of this technique is that the nonverbal right side of the brain is allowed to express itself in words—the language of the left brain. In this way there is communication between both hemispheres, rational and emotional, logical and intuitive. There is also a link between the conscious and the unconscious mind as you will discover in doing these exercises.

I have also found that writing from the right brain (with the nondominant hand) is an excellent way to decode spontaneous art from the unconscious. We do not analyze and intellectualize when we write with the other hand. Instead, this kind of writing reaches into deeper levels of feeling and knowing within ourselves. As you experience this method, you will find out for yourself how simple, yet profound, it is.

THE ROOTS OF ILLNESS

It has long been known that our minds have the power to make us sick or make us well. This is an ancient truth that is now being validated by leading researchers in mind/body healing. We now have scientific verification for the familiar phrases, "She worried herself sick," and "He was worried to death."

Perhaps the most important medical discovery in recent years is that the mind controls the immune system. This finding comes from the emerging science of psychoneuroimmunology (PNI).

One of the leaders in this research is Joan Borysenko, Ph.D., cofounder of the New England Deaconess Hospital Mind/Body Clinic. Dr. Borysenko, formerly of Harvard Medical School, is the author of the best-selling book, *Minding the Body, Mending the Mind.* In her clinical work she has observed

> . . . *a rich and intricate two-way communication system linking the mind, the immune system, and potentially all others systems, a pathway through which our emotions—our hopes and fears—can affect the body's ability to defend itself.*

In the same vein, oncologist Bernie Siegel, M.D., author of the ground-breaking book *Love, Medicine, and Miracles*, writes:

> *We don't yet understand all the ways in which brain chemicals are related to emotions and thoughts, but the salient point is that our state of mind has an immediate and direct effect on our state of body. We can change the body by dealing with how we feel. If we ignore our despair, the body receives a 'die' message. If we deal with our pain and seek help, then the message is 'Living is difficult but desirable,' and the immune system works to keep us alive.*

In counseling people with cancer and AIDS, as well as those suffering from chronic fatigue, Epstein-Barr virus, and candidiasis, I have observed the awesome power and cumulative effect of negative thinking. Patients who keep reinforcing worst-case scenarios in their minds and their conversations weaken both their faith and their determination to recover. Through their thoughts and language they actually dig a pit of helplessness and self-pity that further weakens the immune system and the body's ability to recover. On the other hand, I have seen the equally awesome power of healing through a change in beliefs, mental pictures, and attitudes.

I am now going to share with you a composite case study drawn from my work with many clients. I have heard so many variations on this theme that I privately refer to it as the "sick and tired syndrome."

Our client "Tracy" is an attractive young woman in her late thirties and a successful businesswoman. She has been referred by her best friend, a former client of mine, who is concerned about Tracy's health. Tracy starts our counseling session by describing her chronic fatigue and a variety of symptoms. A fair-complexioned natural blonde, she has lost all color in her face and has dark circles under her eyes. She has always been slender, but has lost a great deal of weight and can now be described as gaunt. She is beside herself with anxiety, and her speech is filled with negative affirmations: "No one is able to help me. . . . I feel terrible all the time. . . . I've tried everything and nothing works. . . . No matter what I do, things go from bad to worse."

Tracy continues with a litany of symptoms: indigestion, food allergies, backaches, headaches, chronic vaginal and bladder infections, fatigue, and depression. She has been to countless doctors, chiropractors, homeopaths, therapists, channelers, and psychics. She has spent a small fortune on medications, treatments, and remedies, and a larger fortune on medical tests and diagnostic workups. She has been diagnosed as having chronic fatigue syndrome, scoliosis, and premenstrual syndrome. She also has chronic digestive problems that have contributed to her weight loss.

When she is not working long hours, Tracy is frantically running all over the city in a desperate attempt to be cured. But her condition has continued to deteriorate. Tracy is worried, nervous, and fearful, and this is expressing itself in her body. As Tracy finishes her story I cannot help but be reminded of philosopher Blaise Pascal's words: "All the unhappiness of men arises from one single fact, that they cannot stay quietly in their own chambers."

I tell Tracy about my own healing journey and how I recovered from a life-threatening collagen disease. I explain the therapeutic value of spontaneous art. She seems encouraged and willing to begin. I start by guiding her on a journey through her body in which she listens to her own physical sensations. I then offer her felt pens and crayons and invite her to draw this experience on paper. Following this, Tracy writes a dialogue with her body. In subsequent sessions Tracy discovers the mental and emotional roots of her physical condition: brutal self-criticism and low self-esteem. Tracy was raised in a family of hard-driving high achievers. In this perfectionistic environment she learned to judge herself mercilessly at an early age. Nothing was ever good enough. She later married a supersuccessful professional whose addictive personality and workaholic lifestyle left her feeling continually abandoned.

After many years she finally got a divorce. However, frightened of being alone, she promptly entered another destructive relationship with an older, semi-retired man who had plenty of time to spend with her. There was only one problem—he smothered her with emotional demands and criticism. From the beginning of this relationship she started developing symptoms; her body seemed to be rebelling against the verbal abuse and judgment her mind was willing to tolerate.

Now, Tracy comes to realize that the treatment she received in these relationships—first abandonment and then criticism—is merely a reflection of how she treats herself and her own body. She is confronted by her own demon, perfectionism, that had enabled her to be a "successful professional" with an expensive car, designer clothes, and a luxurious home. She discovers that the very same perfectionism that propelled her into worldly success is now endangering her health. Tracy finally sees that she has been approaching her quest for a cure with the same driven quality that she brings to her career and relationships. Carl Jung said: "The highest and most decisive experience is to be alone. Only this experience can give one an indestructible foundation." What Tracy needs most—self-nurturing, rest, and quiet—is what she is getting least.

With encouragement and the right tools, Tracy is able to access her Inner Healer. In written dialogues it tells her that she is "running herself ragged." In order to heal, she needs time off from work and from her hectic schedule of medical appointments. As a result she gives herself a week of vacation *alone*—no boyfriend and no telephone. During this quiet period of self-reflection she takes walks on the beach, meditates, and draws and writes out her feelings. She also indulges herself in relaxing massages, afternoon naps, and simply "doing nothing."

At the end of this week, Tracy reports, "I feel better than I have in months." She now believes in her ability to influence her own health for the better. From that time on, Tracy's healing process takes on the quality of a magical adventure. She limits herself to in-depth treatment with one health practitioner whom she trusts, instead of using the "cafeteria" approach. She identifies her core negative beliefs, such as, "I'm not good enough," "I'll be okay if I work harder," "My relationships with men never work out," and "Life is a struggle."

Tracy sees that her destructive beliefs have filtered down to affect her emotions and her body. She then decides to successfully recreate a positive, life-affirming belief system. She does this by creating new pictures on paper and in her mind's eye of how she wants to feel about her body, herself, and her life. She then gives voice to these new images with written affirmations: "My life is joyful," "My relationships are mutually supportive and nurturing," and "I enjoy vibrant health." As she replaces her

Changing negative pictures into positive pictures.

negative beliefs and gloomy pictures of life with a new vision, her health continues to improve dramatically.

This leads to many changes in Tracy's outer life. She breaks up with her boyfriend, and with the help of a women's support group, she is able to face life on her own. She reduces her work schedule and gives herself time for leisure and nurturing friends. During her relationship she had dropped her own friends and become isolated. She also discovers her playful and creative Inner Child through classes in improvisational theater and dance.

Later, Tracy weaves this magical experience back into her professional work, which becomes more playful and creative. Healing becomes an adventure in self-discovery rather than a frantic search for rescue. Most importantly, after years of offering compassion and understanding to clients and others in need, Tracy finally learns to nurture and love herself. With more self-respect, she makes healthier choices in her relationships.

TOOLS FOR HEALING

I wish all physicians would add a box of crayons to their diagnostic and therapeutic tools.
—Bernie S. Siegel, M.D.
Peace, Love & Healing

In order to do the activities in this book, you will need your own "black bag" of art supplies containing the following materials:

Felt pens in assorted colors of eight or more
Unlined white paper (8-1/2" x 11")
Some possibilities are a spiral-bound notebook, a hardbound blank book, or a three-ring notebook with unlined paper
50 loose sheets of inexpensive white paper (8-1/2" x 11")
Newsprint (18" x 24"), 12 sheets (art supply or stationery store)
Scissors and glue (preferably white milk glue)
Magazines with a variety of photographs such as *Life, Vogue, National Geographic, Better Homes and Gardens, Omni*
Crayons or pastels in assorted colors (optional)
Cassette tape player (optional)

HOW TO USE THIS BOOK

The activities presented in this book are meant to be tools. They work only if you use them. How often you use them is up to you. It is not necessary to do them every day to receive benefit. Please avoid turning this into "schoolwork" that you *have* to do. That attitude could lead you to beat yourself up emotionally for not doing it, and then you might never do the activities.

After each exercise is explained, examples of art done by myself or my clients and students are provided. Please be sure to look at these before you begin each activity, as they will help you both understand the processes involved and give you permission to create whatever you need to.

I trust that you will know when to do these activities and how much to do at any given time. The Inner Life flows in rhythms and cycles. There are times when we crave more solitude and self-reflection, and we make time for it. There are times when we seem to need less. However, I do encourage everyone to make some time for themselves each day. In both my personal and my professional life, I have observed that without daily quiet time I run the risk of losing myself. We forget what we need and want and defer to the demands of the outer world. This lack of quiet time is a major cause of stress.

A ROOM OF YOUR OWN

The method presented in this book involves a highly personal process. It requires concentration in a safe atmosphere, free from distraction and the critical eyes of the world. Find a quiet, comfortable place where you can be alone for uninterrupted periods of time without feeling pressured or hurried. Some of these activities will take approximately 15 minutes, others will take longer.

These activities may bring up sensitive issues and feelings. I urge you to keep your drawings and writings confidential and store them in a private place. Be selective in sharing. Show your work only to sympathetic friends, loved ones, health practitioners, or support groups. Avoid sharing with people who are critical. Healing does not take place in an atmosphere of judgment and disapproval.

I suggest two approaches in using this book. The first is to read the entire book through before doing any of the activities. The other approach is to stop and do each activity as you read the text. No matter which style you prefer, please *do the activities in the sequence they are presented,* for each one builds upon the skills and confidence learned in the previous exercises.

You are now ready to embark upon your own personal adventure to become the *picture of health.*

2

Thinking and Feeling on Paper

Although I was a professional artist, when I started scribbling my feelings out while ill with the collagen disease, my art training gave me no advantage. In fact, I was hampered by all that training and professional skill. I was used to making art that "looked good," art that people paid for: greeting cards, posters, magazine covers. The emotionally expressive art that I did when I was ill looked so strange to me that I feared my sanity had been affected by the disease. The drawings looked nothing like my typical style. They seemed primitive, surrealistic, and indecipherable to my literal mind. Even though I had done both abstract and representational art in the past, I had no frame of reference for these mysterious drawings from the unconscious. And a critical voice in my mind started yelling at me for doing such "ugly" art. It berated me for wasting my time on drawings that had no income-producing or aesthetic merit whatsoever.

I also noticed that the process by which I did these spontaneous drawings was totally different from the way I approached my professional art. When I designed greeting cards, I used to get a rough mental picture, sketch it out, and then create the final artwork. In contrast, my drawings from the unconscious practically drew themselves on the paper. They seemed to come out of my heart and guts rather than my head. At times, I felt as if my hand was doing the drawing on its own, similar to the descriptions I had heard about automatic writing. In fact, one could describe this therapeutic art as a kind of "automatic drawing."

I tell you this story about my own discovery of art as therapy because it is so easy for "nonartists" to become intimidated about doing any kind of art. I want you to know that a trained artist has no advantage when it comes to art as therapy. The goal of therapeutic art is entirely different from that of fine art or commercial art. In fine art and commercial art the goal is to create a product for the response and appreciation of

19

others. *In therapeutic art the product or end goal is the self-discovery process of the individual making the art.* When it comes to art as therapy, we are all on equal footing.

Visual art is a language of colors, shapes, and lines. It is a language of its own. It is especially powerful for communicating feelings and intuitions that go beyond words. There are some feelings and inner experiences that simply cannot be expressed in verbal language.

Literacy is usually defined as the ability to read and write. There is an equivalent in the language of art: *visual literacy.* Visual literacy is the ability to "read" art, understand it, appreciate it, and feel it. Visual literacy also includes the ability to make art for aesthetic decoration, communication, or therapy. Millions of people in our society consider themselves literate. It is generally accepted that almost anyone can be taught to read and write. That belief is the cornerstone of public compulsory education. Literacy is not a question of talent or creativity, but a matter of training. On the other hand, most people think they do not have the ability to draw. They believe that drawing is for people who have "talent," a mysterious ingredient (presumably in the genes) that one is either born with or lacks altogether. This is simply not true.

We all have the ability to draw until we are taught otherwise. This ability is a universal human characteristic. It is this same ability which enables us to write. So, if you can write, you can draw. If you can read, you can become visually literate. The fact is that visual art is far older than written words: drawing came before writing.

For many years I was a Head Start supervisor and instructor of child development on the college level. I observed thousands of children throughout the country from various ethnic and socioeconomic backgrounds. I discovered that all preschool-age children draw naturally with spontaneity and exuberance.

You do not have to study art history in order to understand the role of visual art in the evolution of literacy. One can observe this in children today. Before they ever learn to print or write, they scribble and doodle spontaneously. No one has to show them how. Give any toddler a piece of paper and a crayon or pencil, and a scribble will result. If the child has never watched someone draw or write, it may be necessary to demonstrate that the writing tool will leave marks on the paper. What a great discovery for a young child!

Sometime in the second or third year, with no instruction, that same child starts representing objects on paper. The scribbles now become "people": circles with dots for eyes and a line for a mouth. Later, these "people" may have two lines dangling down from the circular head: legs. These forms often resemble pollywogs. And still later, a body shape might appear between the circle (head) and the two lines (legs and feet). "Houses" are composed of angles and straight lines (triangles, rectangles, or squares). As children draw, they often talk about what they are drawing: "This is Gramma" or "That's my doggie, Poodles."

This process is actually the beginning of writing. The child understands the concept of visual symbol making (marks on paper which "stand for" something else). Unfortunately, once we left nursery school or kindergarten, where scribbling was tolerated, and entered the world of reading, writing and arithmetic, art took a back seat (except on rainy days and holidays). I was one of the lucky ones who survived. My Inner Artist was recognized and encouraged by family and teachers. But I was also seen as "different" from the other children: one of the "talented" ones.

Sadly, we have forgotten visual literacy in our culture, and most believe they cannot make art, so they do not. I have witnessed this over the years with my students and clients. Again and again, I have heard the vast majority say they "can't draw" and "don't have any talent." Most of them get very nervous and fidgety when I tell them we are going to draw. They start giggling like teenagers and apologize *before they ever begin to draw.*

In discussions we usually find the roots of the "I can't draw" belief: A teacher, parent, sibling, or some authority figure had ridiculed the individual's early attempts at drawing. A verdict had been delivered: no talent. Or, it had been considered frivolous or "sissy" to engage in artistic activities. That was the end of art for most. After all, who wants to be criticized and made fun of? Did that ever happen to you? If so, you are not alone.

However, there is something you can do about it. It is never too late to become visually literate, to learn the language of art. The activities in this chapter introduce you to art as a therapeutic tool. You will learn how drawing can be a healing experience. It does not matter whether or not you think you have talent. There is nothing to compete for, no right or wrong way, no good or bad drawings. You cannot possibly make a mistake! There are no standards to live up to and no judgments from outside.

In this chapter you will be expressing emotions with color on paper—something every child knows how to do but most adults have forgotten. This is a safe and playful way to let off steam and release stress.

Let us begin with the most basic mode of drawing: scribbling, doodling, and making marks on paper. We are not attempting to make symbols here. There is no intention to make a "pleasing" picture or a recognizable depiction of the three-dimensional world.

EXERCISE: PLAYING ON PAPER

Purpose: Learning to relax and enjoy making marks on paper without expectations; enjoying the process of exploring with colors.

Materials: Plain white, unlined paper, crayons or felt pens.

Choose colors that feel good to you by following your instincts. With your dominant hand (the one you normally write with) make marks, doodles, scribbles, or shapes on paper. Keep it simple. Do not try to make a picture or symbol of anything. Do not use any words.

Continue playing with color, using as many pieces of paper as you wish.

Repeat the steps above but use your nondominant hand (the one you do not normally write with).

The following are three pairs of playful drawings. In each set, the first drawing was done with the dominant hand and the second with the nondominant hand.

"Playing on Paper":
Using Dominant Hand

"Playing on Paper":
Using Nondominant Hand

"Playing on Paper":
Using Dominant Hand

"Playing on Paper":
Using Nondominant Hand

"Playing on Paper":
Using Dominant Hand

"Playing on Paper":
Using Nondominant Hand

Drawing can be a wonderful form of meditation. The act of focusing and shutting out external distractions through art can be very calming and centering. In the following meditative drawing exercise, you will practice staying in the moment. You will be experiencing the page in front of you as a world unto itself, just as artists do. It is best to take your time and go slowly with this type of drawing. Think of the blank paper as a meditative mind with visual thoughts floating across it.

DRAWING AS MEDITATION

Purpose: Learning to use drawing as a meditation for relaxing and clearing the mind; allowing yourself to enjoy the moment with no expectations or pressure to perform.

Materials: Felt pens, crayons, pencils, or pastels; several sheets of white paper.

Choose whatever color attracts you. Allow your hand to move across the page, drawing whatever it wants to. Do not premeditate or plan what the drawing will look like. Let your hand feel its way around the page, drawing spontaneously. Allow images to emerge. If your mind wanders to thoughts of other things, just stop, go back to the present moment, and focus on the paper. Stay with your experience of the colors, lines, shapes, and textures your hand is making on the paper.

Do as many meditative drawings as you wish. Try using your "other hand" for some of them.

The series of drawings illustrating this exercise, all done with the non-dominant hand, demonstrates the great variety of styles which emerge from this simple activity. The differences in style are as obvious as the differences one observes in people's handwriting.

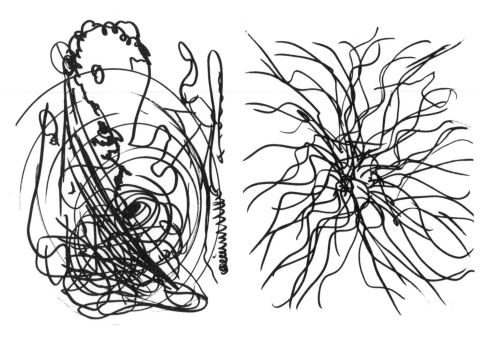

Drawing as Meditation   *Drawing as Meditation*

Drawing as Meditation

Drawing as Meditation

BEYOND WORDS

Think
of
MIRO
ov
Kandinsky

→

Drawing is a form of emotional expression that can reach places where words cannot go. There are some feelings and moods that simply cannot be translated into neat little phrases or sentences. At those times we are "speechless." We feel something but we have no words for it. Our mood defies description.

Because we have been trained to label things (and thereby control them), this speechless mode can be extremely uncomfortable. We may actually ignore the feelings because we do not have words for them. But the feelings do not go away. They have energy. They may fester in the dark. They may hide out in our bodies only to appear later as symptoms of physical or emotional illness. Although many people have experienced music as a wonderful way to express feelings, it is less known that drawing can do the same.

In the next exercise you will learn to express feelings in colors, lines, shapes, and textures on paper.

DRAWING WITH FEELING

Purpose: Learning to express feelings in the language of graphic art; tapping into your right brain through your nondominant hand.

Materials: Separate sheets of plain white paper and colored felt pens. Pastels or crayons are also recommended for this exercise.

Sit quietly for a moment. Tune in to your feelings and allow yourself to experience them fully. If your feelings had a color, what would it be? Do your feelings seem to have a shape? If your feelings could make sounds, what would they be? What kind of rhythm would they have? Is there a scent associated with your feelings? Do your feelings have a texture or a pattern? Are they hot or cold?

Now draw your feelings out on paper. Choose the colors that feel right for you. Allow yourself to draw spontaneously without judgment or concern for the finished product. Let your drawing be a process—have fun exploring and experimenting. Your picture does not have to look like anything in the outer world. It's okay to scribble, doodle, and make abstract shapes, lines, and patterns. Let your drawing be an outward expression of your inner world.

Number and label your drawings. Make as many drawings of feelings as you wish.

After you have completed your drawings, arrange them in the order you drew them and look at them. Observe the feeling tone and the changes from one drawing to another.

The next time you are dealing with difficult feelings, perhaps sadness, anger, frustration, or confusion, scribble them out on paper as you did in this exercise.

The following sequence of seven drawings illustrates a wide array of feelings "pictured" on paper.

Feelings 1

Feelings 2

Feelings 3

Feelings 4

The woman who did this drawing is a schoolteacher. She expressed her delight that summer vacation had arrived. Yippee!

Anger

This drawing was done by Eve over a period of several days. She portrayed her feelings each day in a separate section of the design. You can see the contrast in the tone of her feelings from one area to another.

The following two drawings were done by Sondra, who decided to draw one with her dominant hand and the other with her nondominant hand.

"Drawing with Feeling": Using Dominant Hand

"Drawing with Feeling": Using Nondominant Hand

DRAWING YOUR STRESS OUT

My clinical experience has shown me that stress is a major factor in physical illness and emotional pain. Rush-hour traffic, job deadlines, overdue bills, and family crises are only a few of the common situations associated with stress. Sometimes we need a simple release of the tension that builds up when living in a fast-paced world.

When I was a child development supervisor, I learned an important lesson from preschool children in our Head Start program. These children were black, Latino, and Asian, living in Los Angeles in 1965, the year of the Watts riots. Talk about tension and stress! War was being waged in the streets of these children's very own neighborhoods. I noticed that one way they were able to express their feelings of anger, fear, and sadness was through scribbling and drawing with crayons. It was a safe way to let their feelings out without hurting others or the environment. I have never forgotten the relief and calmness on their faces, as well as in their body language; through art we had given them a safe place to feel their feelings, express themselves, and be accepted just the way they were.

Many years later, when I was in graduate training to be an art therapist, I found myself feeling very stressed out. Suddenly I remembered those Head Start children. I got myself a big box of thick crayons and started scribbling my feelings. I could feel my tension releasing and flowing right out onto the paper. It was a tremendous relief and I did it often after that, usually ending the sessions with laughter. I often scrawled four-letter words and felt like a rebellious teenager making graffiti, except that I was doing it in my own private journal rather then defacing public property. Indeed, it stands to reason that if teenagers were given the opportunity to express their feelings in art classes or workshops, there might be a lot less graffiti on our public buildings.

GRAFFITI DRAWING

Purpose: Learning to release stress through drawing.

Materials: Felt pens or crayons, several sheets of paper.

The next time you find yourself in a stressful situation, as soon as possible take the opportunity to draw it out by scribbling and making marks on paper. Keep these drawings abstract and choose colors that express how you feel about the situation. Use as many sheets of paper as you need.

These three graffiti scribbles show how "getting things off your chest" on paper can bring great relief.

Oftentimes we feel like victims of circumstance, powerless to change certain areas of our lives. We think we will never get our bodies into shape, have the fulfilling relationship we want, have a satisfying job, or get our finances in order. We not only fill our conversation with these negative statements, but we also fill our minds with negative mental pictures. These become self-fulfilling prophecies. The more we rerun those old "soap operas" in our minds and the more we use them in our speech, and the more we act them out in our lives.

The next exercise demonstrates that you *can* repicture your life the way you want it.

UN-STRESSING

Purpose: Identifying stressful situations; changing the picture from a negative to a positive one.

Materials: Crayons, felt pens, paper.

Draw a diagram or symbolic picture of a stressful situation. What does it look like? What does it feel like? Do you feel trapped in a box? Overwhelmed by a mountain of work? Attacked by daggers of criticism? Create a graphic metaphor that shows your experience of the situation. Do as many drawings as you wish until you capture the situation on paper.

Now draw a picture of *how you would like the situation to feel*. How can you change the negative picture into a positive one? For instance, if you drew yourself under a mountain of work, you might now show yourself sitting contentedly on top of the mountain of completed work.

Here are examples of "before" and "after" drawings. First, Jane Murphy pictured the overview of her life as a pattern of doodles and scribbles. It felt too busy and chaotic to her, so she redrew the picture showing how she wanted her life to feel. About her second picture she wrote: "This feels better to me because it is more simple. I love simple things. They make so much sense to me."

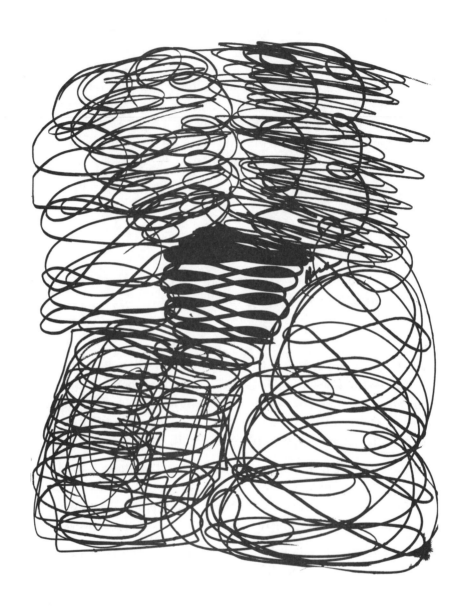

MOVEMENT, MUSIC, AND DRAWING

In my workshops on creativity, I often lead participants through an experiment involving movement and drawing. First I have them do the "Drawing with Feeling" exercise that I presented earlier. Then I have them do some spontaneous movement to various types of music. I call this "Find Your Own Dance." No structured dance steps are allowed: no fox trots or waltzes, no twists or jerks or whatever the current dance craze is. Each individual is asked to find and improvise his or her own movement. Sometimes I ask everyone to close their eyes so that they will not be self-conscious about how they appear to others, or be distracted by what others are doing.

After we do the "Find Your Own Dance" activity, I have them repeat the drawing exercise. The results are always astonishing. The drawings done after the movement activity are much freer, relaxed, and colorful. And people invariably report that they had more fun doing the second set of drawings. They had loosened up and gotten into a more playful mood, and it showed in the drawings.

In my art education classes at a local college, I often did drawing exercises accompanied by music. I would present the "Scribbling" exercise and ask each student to do several drawings. Then I would play a recorded musical medley while they produced several more drawings. I would encourage them to respond to the rhythm and feeling of the music through their drawing—to think of the paper as a dance floor, a place to really let go and play. Later we would compare the two sets of drawings. The drawings done to music contained more life and energy, with strokes and colors that reflected exuberance and self-confidence.

After doing these exercises the class would discuss how the music had affected them while they were drawing. Some common responses were:

> "I stopped worrying about how the drawing looked and concentrated more on the feelings in my body."

> "At first, the music just relaxed me so that I was not so uptight and critical of what I was drawing. Then I got so much into the music that

*it felt like I was ice skating again the way I did when I was a kid. It
was really fun. I did not think I could enjoy drawing."*

*"The music seemed to wash through me and determine the patterns
I made on the paper. When it was staccato, I used repeating strokes or
dots; when it was melodic, my hand made circles and figure eights."*

*"I found myself interpreting the music through the colors I chose and
the amount of pressure I used. With the up-tempo jazz, I drew with
more pressure and brighter or darker colors. I also drew with crayons
so that I could press harder. When the lyrical music came on, I wanted
the pastels. The colors were softer, but so was the material. And I could
blend the colors gently with my fingers and that motion really seemed
to express the softness of the music (which was by Debussy)."*

*"The music took my mind off my expectations of how the drawing
should turn out. I got into the colors and the sounds and forgot about
my mental thoughts."*

Drawing to music tends to keep you in the *present* instead of the future,
in the *process* instead of the outcome. It definitely gets you out of your
left (logical/verbal) brain and into your right (visual/spatial) brain. Also,
this is a very kinesthetic approach to drawing, in which you use your
whole body, not just your arms, hands, and eyes.

One of my workshop participants was so excited by these experiments
that she introduced me to her music instructor, Alexandra Pierce, who
was doing the same kind of exercises with piano students. As a guest at
Pierce's class, I watched as she instructed each student to play a short
solo piece for the class. This was followed by a long session in which she
led the class through spontaneous movement and dance exercises. The
class ended with each student once again playing a brief solo for the class.

The contrast was so great between the "before movement" and "after
movement" piano solos that it hardly seemed like the same people playing. The first solos were technically proficient, but rather dull. The second
time the solos were alive! The students really moved and put their bodies
into the music. As a result, the music was richer and more colorful. There

was also a remarkable difference in "stage presence." This is a very important factor for performing artists. I had a wonderful time comparing notes (no pun intended) with Pierce on our teaching methods and sharing the universal principles we had used in our respective fields.

Now it's your turn to have fun with movement, music, and drawing.

DRAWING TO MUSIC

Purpose: Combining auditory and kinesthetic expression with visual art experience; relaxing into drawing through movement to music.

Materials: Large sheets of newsprint paper (18″ x 24″); felt pens, crayons, or pastels in assorted colors.

Music of your choice, preferably expressing a variety of moods and tempos.

In a place where you can be completely alone, do some spontaneous movement to music. Allow your *body* to respond to the music, not your critical mind that wants to look good or acceptable to others. Listen to the music with your whole body, improvising and playing with the rhythm and the melody. If you find yourself reverting back to structured or traditional dance steps, just be aware of it and go back to improvising and finding your own dance. Do this for a few minutes or as long as you like.

As you continue playing the music, take your art materials and start drawing to the music. Let it flow through you. Use colors that you associate with the sounds and rhythms. Express any feelings that are evoked by the music. If you have more than one medium, choose the appropriate one for a particular musical passage; i.e., it may be easier to interpret one piece of music with crayons, and another with felt pens. Make as many drawings to music as you wish.

Drawing to Music

Drawing to Music

Drawing to Music

Drawing to Music

3

Are You In Your Body?

Mr. Dufy lived a short distance from his body.
—James Joyce

You have probably met people who, like Mr. Dufy, do not seem to inhabit their bodies. You have heard people described as "living in their heads," "spaced out," "not present."

Where do *you* live: in your whole body, or just in your head? For many in our Western culture the body is simply a pedestal on which to rest the head. We have glorified the rational mind at the expense of the body. We speak of mind *over* matter instead of mind *in* matter. This split is epitomized in Descartes' proclamation, "I think, therefore I am." We define ourselves as thinkers who happen to inhabit a physical form.

The reason many of us become ill is because we habitually live in our thoughts, memories, and fantasies, disconnected from the experience of our bodies. As absentee landlords we have abandoned our homes (our bodies) in favor of a world of the mind. Obviously this creates a dilemma. How can the body get our attention?

Through pain and disease. In this way it sends out a desperate plea for help. When it has been ignored this is often its only means for bringing us "down to earth" and "back to our senses."

ILLNESS AS TEACHER

I don't believe that a person actually creates disease, but that his soul is expressing an important message through the disease.

—Arnold Mindell
Working with the Dreaming Body

We often look at the symptoms of illness as bearers of bad tidings to be silenced or ignored. This chapter offers an alternative view—a method for *using symptoms as guides* to find a gold mine of wisdom hidden within yourself. It contains techniques for tapping into your natural, innate power to heal yourself.

This chapter will show you how to listen to your body, and to appreciate the role of pain and other physical symptoms as teachers in your life. You will see how your physical body mirrors your thoughts and feelings, and you will be given techniques for uncovering the roots of illness in your own beliefs and attitudes. As you embrace the very things you fear—pain and other symptoms—you will discover that they contain valuable messages from the Inner Healer. Dr. Albert Schweitzer referred to this Inner Healer as the "doctor within."

THE SYMPTOM LEADS TO THE CURE

As an art therapist who has worked clinically with hundreds of patients struggling with chronic or life-threatening illness, I have no doubt that our inner wisdom speaks through physical symptoms. I have observed countless individuals discover that their symptoms were precise metaphors for aspects of their lives that needed healing.

For instance, Kim was having serious problems with her eyesight. In drawings and written dialogues with her eyes she learned that there were some problems in her marriage that she "didn't want to see." She started to look at herself and her own needs more truthfully, and stopped blaming her husband for her problems. Her vision began to improve as she communicated her "insights" more openly with her husband.

The symptom, as a carrier of messages from the Inner Healer, is actually a great ally in maintaining balance and health. A symptom is a reminder. It says: "Pay attention! You're neglecting something. Your needs are not being met." When something has been "disowned" or repressed in our lives, sometimes the only way the Inner Healer can get us to listen is through pain and illness.

Jason was a workaholic who suffered from chronic low-back pain. Believing he had to do everything himself, he was in the habit of carrying a huge load of "back-breaking" responsibilities. To him, asking for help or taking time off were signs of weakness, and weakness was "bad." He had to be strong and self-sufficient at any cost. But the cost was high. Ironically, the very weakness he had feared and disowned showed up in his lower back. The pain had become so severe that his doctors were recommending surgery.

He attended one of my "Finding the Healer Within" workshops. When he drew pictures of his back pain, he got the message. The picture included captions that said, "Help! I need rest!" He understood that his symptom was forcing him to take the rest he would not take voluntarily. Jason started delegating some work to others so he could take some time off. He began visiting a desert spa, sitting in therapeutic mineral pools, and learning to relax. By listening to what his pain was *really* saying and responding to his body's needs, he began to feel better.

Focusing on a physical symptom with the right techniques allows the unconscious to speak. The emotions that have been stuffed in the body part begin to tumble out. The mental beliefs that have been lodged in the body begin to reveal themselves. One discovers the Inner Wisdom communicating through physical symptoms.

In the exercises that follow, you will be given tools for communicating directly with your body, your feelings, and your beliefs and attitudes. The illustrations that accompany the exercises will demonstrate the simplicity, drama, and power of this process.

BODY SENSING

In this exercise, you will learn to focus your awareness inside your own body through sensory meditation. You will be guided on a personal inventory of your current physical symptoms and sensations. As you follow this exercise your attention will move through every part of your body, from the tips of your toes to the top of your head.

Sit comfortably on a chair with your spine straight. Relax and focus your attention on your breathing. Follow the rhythm of the breath and allow it to become deeper and slower. Experience yourself being nourished as you take in the breath of life. With your eyes closed, continue to focus on your breathing. Inhale and exhale for ten cycles.

Do the "Body Sensing" meditation slowly and with full awareness. Check to see if there is pain or discomfort in any area of your body. Start by paying attention to your left foot: the toes, the sole, and the heel. Slowly move your awareness to the top of your foot and up your leg: ankle, calf, knee, thigh, buttock, and hip joint. Repeat this process on your right side.

Now, move through your torso, beginning with the pelvic area and the genitals. Continue moving up your spine, through your lower, middle, and upper back. Now, move up the front of your body: the abdominal region, rib cage, and chest. Check out all of the sensations inside your body.

Now, shift your awareness to the fingers of your left hand and move up the hand to your wrist. Continue moving up through your forearm, elbow, upper arm, and shoulder. Repeat the same process on your right side.

Now focus your attention on your neck and throat. Move to your face: chin and jaw, mouth, nose, cheeks, eyes, ears, and forehead. Check out the sensations inside your mouth and throat, your nose, and ears. Now place your awareness on your skull. Move your attention from the hairline around your face to the top of the head, down the back to the base of your skull at the neck. Complete this "Body Sensing" meditation by moving to a still point at the center of your head between the left and right hemispheres of the brain.

BODY PICTURING

Purpose: Identifying the physical sensations and symptoms you ex-
            perienced in the Body Sensing Meditation and expressing
            them through color on paper.

Materials: Notebook with unlined paper or individual sheets of paper.
            Felt pens, crayons, colored pencils, or pastels in assorted
            colors.

You will now draw a picture of your body based on the experience you
had during the "Body Sensing" meditation. Using your nondominant
hand, create an outline of your body.* Then color in the areas where you
felt strong sensations during the meditation. Choose colors that express
the nature of the sensations you felt. For instance, if a particular part of
your body felt numb or cold, select a color that you associate with that
specific sensation. You may also color in areas *around* the body if that
seems appropriate. Use your nondominant hand for the entire drawing.

*If you normally write with your right hand, use your left hand. If you are a left-
handed writer, use your right hand.

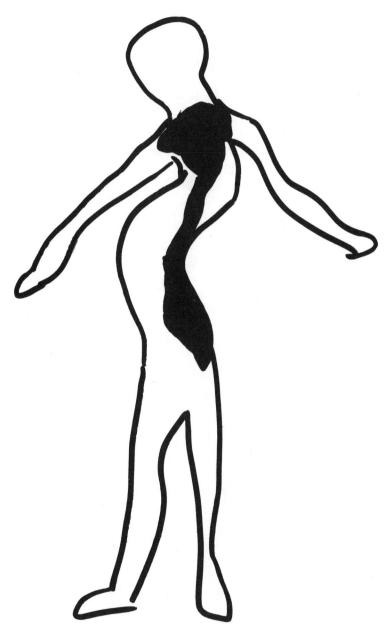

Body Picturing

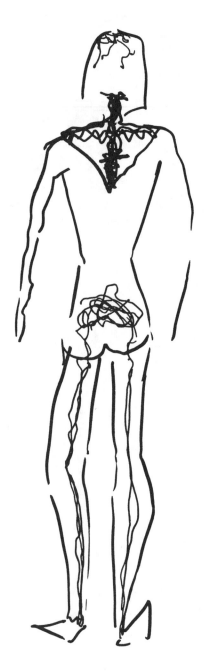

Body Picturing

The following exercise will enable you to actually converse with the parts of your body that are talking through the symptoms you mapped out in the "Body Picturing" exercise. In the "Body Talking" exercise, you will give voice to your physical sensations. What is more, you will get to the unconscious psychological roots of the pain or discomfort, and then uncover specific needs. Later, you will be shown how to meet these needs in order to heal yourself.

BODY TALKING

Purpose: Discovering the psychological aspects of physical pain and discomfort; finding out what the body needs in order to feel better.

Materials: Colored felt pens, paper.

In this activity, the drawing you did in the "Body Picturing" exercise will "come to life" and talk to you. You will be writing with both hands. Your dominant hand will be the interviewer, your nondominant hand will write the response as it "speaks" for the body and its symptoms.

Your nondominant hand will write in the same colors used in the earlier drawing for each body part. Your dominant hand will write in a contrasting color.

With your dominant hand, write the following questions:

1. Who are you?
2. How do you feel today?
3. Why do you feel this way?
4. How can I help you?

Allow the body part to write its response with the nondominant hand. It will probably be slow and awkward. Be patient and take your time. There are strong emotions living in the body. These emotions are seeking expression.

If you wish, read the following dialogue before attempting your own. They will help you understand how this process can work when you allow your body to speak uncensored.

The next illustration and dialogue were done by Christy in one of my workshops. Her drawing shows many body parts in need of attention. She wrote dialogues with each area and received clear guidance on how to heal herself. Upon responding to the needs expressed in her dialogue, Christy experienced tremendous changes in her life. The next time I saw her she looked dramatically different. Her eyes were brighter, she smiled and laughed more, and she expressed a great deal of confidence in her ability to deal with difficult situations. She reported that these exercises have become an important part of her growth and healing process.

CHRISTY'S DIALOGUE

R: Who are you?

L: I am your voice and I want to be heard!

R: Who are you?

L: I am your genitals and I want to be touched!

R: And who else?

L: I am your arms and I want to be filled.

R: Voice, how are you?

L: I come and I go. I feel pressure like hands around me.

R: Genitals, how are you?

L: We are tired of being alone. We are lonely.

R: Arms, how are you?

L: We are empty. It doesn't feel good.

R: Voice, why do you feel that way?

L: Because I'm scared if I say who I am no one will like me.

R: Genitals, why do you feel that way?

L: Because we are scared. We always pick the wrong people.

R: Arms, why do you feel that way?

L: Because we don't know how to let go. We always want to hang on forever. This makes us very tired.

R: Voice, what can I do to make you feel better?

L: Speak up! Or no one will get to know who you are. You're very beautiful inside. I want you to _stop_ hiding!

R: Genitals, what can I do to make you feel better?

L: Stop treating us like we were not part of you—like we are separate, from another planet. We are a part of your wholeness and well-beingness.

R: Arms, what can I do to make you feel better?

L: Stop trying to fill me up all the time—let me rest. Don't give me too much to carry all at once.

R: Who are you?

L: I am your back.

R: How do you feel?

L: I feel weak and abused.

R: Why?

L: You don't appreciate me and lift and carry heavy weight of responsibility that should be carried or shared by others. You have always done this even as a little child. You let others give you loads that were far too heavy. They were not even your loads but you carried them. You wanted to please them.

R: How can I help?

L: Learn to say no. Learn to take time for yourself. *Make* time. Quit adjusting to the demands of others. Quit carrying their loads. Stop being everyone's mother. I will yell at you when you don't do this. Stop being so supportive of the works of others and start recognizing the value of your talents.

This drawing and the accompanying "Body Talking" dialogue were done by Sarah in one of my workshops entitled "Finding the Healer Within." As you will see from her dialogue, her problems with her back, neck, and left eye were all signals of unresolved issues in her life. She discovered that her back pain was a symptom of being overburdened, her neck stiffness was a sign that she needed to be more flexible, and her eye problem encouraged her to use her inner vision.

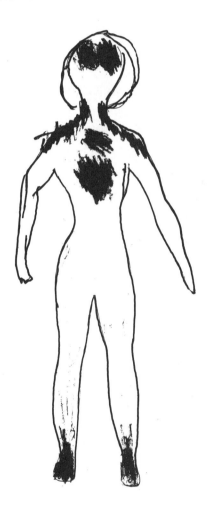

SARAH'S DIALOGUE

R: Who are you?

L: I am your neck.

R: How do you feel?

L: You know I have hurt for ten years.

R: Why?

L: Because you were betrayed by someone you loved and counted on. I became stiff because you were afraid to look around and see what was really going on in your world. You were afraid of the changes that you knew had to come. You were in deep fear so you manifested the girl who hit you and caused the whiplash.

R: What can I do to help?

L: Be more flexible. Take more time to reflect on the direction you want to turn. Quit forcing yourself.

R: Who are you?

L: I am your left eye.

R: How do you feel?

L: Useless and confused.

R: Why?

L: You lost me when you were in confusion and anger and fear.

R: What can I do to help?

L: Let me rest awhile. Use more of your inner vision. Develop it. Let it grow. Nurture it. It will show you more than I ever did. Don't focus on me and one day I'll surprise you.

Ken Johnston's story of healing shows the power of paying attention to the symptoms. In his twelve-year career as a watercolor artist, author, and instructor, Ken had become more and more concerned with painting pictures with commercial appeal. Although he was successful, he had to work hard for a living and it didn't seem particularly fun or fulfilling. As Ken described it:

> *I look back and see now that I was painting and teaching not for me, but for the public and their approval. In doing so I hoped to fill the emptiness inside me. Lack of support for my own artistic/creative needs created a stream that twisted and turned and was often dry. What I needed to develop was self-approval and self-love and a way to find a clear, true course, with full and flowing waters. Paradoxically, I found the way through a debilitating physical condition.*

When Ken's dominant (right) hand, arm, and shoulder suddenly became numb and painful, he slipped into his old denial mechanism: "ignore it and it will go away." But his childhood programming had been very strong. When he felt weakest and most heartsick, a voice inside said, "Come on! Shape up! You've got work to do! Don't be a sissy!" In retrospect, Ken observed that he had become a "self-employed and insensitive slave-driver—who was also the slave."

Instead of slowing down and honoring his own vulnerability, Ken threw himself into more volunteer activities as a church musician, board member of a human rights organization, and chairman of its charity activities. He got so busy that there was no time for dealing with his own needs and pain. Eventually a series of financial disasters and career pressures finally forced him to stop and reflect. As he put it: "My fragile male ego and self-worth were more badly battered and bruised. It felt like the stream not only dried up, it had been bulldozed away."

When he realized that denying his pain was not going to make it go away, Ken started looking for help. Upon resolving to love himself and heal his life, he discovered Louise Hay's book, *You Can Heal Your Life*. It was an important step in his search for health, which had now become the most pressing issue in his life. He sought medical treatment and was diagnosed as having Carpal Tunnel Syndrome. He was instructed to wear a wrist brace and was told that surgery might be necessary.

Ken also sought help through therapeutic massage and nutritional as well as psychological counseling. This was a big breakthrough because he had always subscribed to the popular belief that counseling was for the weak and mentally ill. As he looked inward he realized that he was "tired of shouldering the weight of a career that felt heavy and dead."

Although there was some improvement, Ken was still unable to paint. However, he had learned enough about the body/mind connection to suspect that his creative block was a sign that there were still things to be learned and issues to be addressed. While browsing through a bookstore one day, Ken recalled that a book literally fell off the shelf into his hands. It was my book, *The Power of Your Other Hand: A Course in Channeling the Wisdom of the Right Brain.* He immediately felt a rush and tingle as his eyes were drawn to the cover design which included the words, "I am your *inner child, artist, writer, healer,* and *teacher.*"

After reading the book and doing the drawing and writing exercises with his nondominant (left) hand, Ken said he felt energized and on his way toward healing. He later came to Los Angeles and attended one of my workshops. Through the combination of drawing and written dialogues, as well as the group atmosphere of acceptance and support, he gave himself permission to express his true feelings. He was able to look at the patterns in his life that needed to be changed, and he experienced more love for himself than ever before.

Ken later discovered that the source of his physical block was in his neck—the connecting link between his brain (thoughts) and his heart (feelings). It was obvious that his heart had not been in his artwork or volunteer activities, and his mind and body would not support him in this "loveless" environment. In contacting his heart's desire, Ken discovered a little boy, "Kenny," whose feelings, joy, and creativity had been blocked for so many years.

Ken's earlier artwork was highly representational and could be described as photo-realism. It reflected his outer vision of the world of the senses. As he resumed painting, he called upon "Kenny's" heart, wisdom, and vision to create and express new images, which he calls "heartworks." He thinks of these new images as the work of the "playful spirit that flows in and through him."

Following are examples of Ken's early (top) and current work (bottom).

On Peaceful Waters

Swan Guardian

4

The Picture of Health

As a man thinks, so he becomes. That is the eternal mystery.
—The Upanishads

Since 1973 my study of the healing process has included work with thousands of clients and students. In this research I have observed the same phenomenon over and over again: beliefs and thoughts about ourselves and our world affect our feelings, which in turn affect our bodies.

For instance, when I became ill with the collagen disease, I discovered a strong set of beliefs which had developed unconsciously over a period of years. These beliefs showed up in pictures that I drew of myself: I stood in an earthquake, the earth cracking apart under my feet (no support). In another drawing I was a trapeze artist on a wire that snapped, sending me crashing to the earth (again, no support).

These drawings all made a great deal of sense when I realized that the years leading up to my illness were a time when my old support system had crumbled. The people and the institutions I had always depended upon were not there when I needed them.

So I concluded that I was all alone in the world with no one to rely upon. The beliefs sounded like this:

> *I am alone.*
> *There is no one I can really trust or count on.*
> *I have to do it all myself.*
> *Life is difficult at best, and is often totally overwhelming.*

This attitude severely limited my ability to cope with the stress of dramatic life changes.

The *truth* is, there were plenty of people and resources "waiting in the wings" to help me. I just hadn't opened my eyes yet. Until I allowed a new cast of supporting characters to enter my life, I was trapped in this "I am all alone" belief system.

If you had challenged my beliefs at that time, I would have run down a list of all the people and groups who had let me down or abandoned me in time of need. I would have defended my beliefs to the end. And, of course, these beliefs would have done me in if I had not changed them.

But that is all they were—beliefs. Beliefs that had grown out of distorted interpretations and erroneous conclusions based on my limited life experience. I know now that belief systems create a blueprint that determines what is possible in our lives. But until the time of my illness I did not realize this, and consequently, my personal blueprint was very constricting. It is no accident that my physical condition precisely mirrored the nature of my beliefs. My old life had fallen apart and I felt utterly disconnected from myself and the world. I was suffering from a *degeneration of the connective tissue* (collagen) in the body.

Think about being all alone, isolated, with no one to help you. Imagine you are cut off from love, support, and encouragement. You struggle all on your own to survive and cope with day-to-day problems. What pictures come to mind? What words or phrases would you use to describe your pictures?

Loneliness, isolation, abandonment—this exactly describes my state of mind prior to my illness. These negative, limiting beliefs surfaced during my illness in the form of journal drawings. By seeing these unconscious thought-forms on paper, I realized that they had created a powerful backdrop for my life. Like a stage setting, my negative beliefs had created a tone and mood for my own personal drama. What is more, I became aware of how the negative pictures in my unconscious mind had affected my emotions and body.

In this journal drawing I expressed the loneliness, isolation and abandonment I felt when I became ill. The second drawing shows me coming back to life after speaking my inner truth as represented by the curvilinear lines flowing out of my mouth like a prayer.

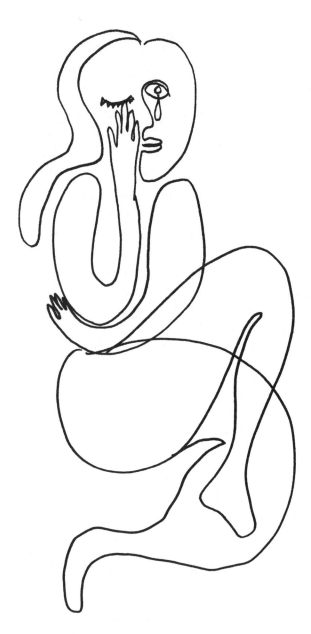

Lonely, Isolated, and Abandoned

Coming Back to Life

THE POWER OF NEGATIVE IMAGES

During those difficult years leading up to the illness, the same abilities that had served me so well as an artist were working against me in my personal life. Why? Because I did not understand that the same faculty that I used in making beautiful art—namely, my creative imagination— was out of control and working destructively in areas such as my relationships, health, and self-esteem. I had allowed negative pictures to form in my mind, to shape my attitudes, to color my feelings, and literally run my life. I was getting results I *did not* want because I was not in charge of my own mind. Like overgrown weeds, these thoughts and beliefs had taken over my inner world and left no room for creative dreams and visions to flourish.

I was able to recognize and challenge my limiting belief system. This process began when I shared my journal drawings with my close friend, Sally. With her support I developed the courage to explore entirely new ways of thinking. I found myself devouring books about personal growth and self-discovery. Sally referred me to a class in which I learned to meditate and use the power of mental imagery. I also learned that the images in our unconscious minds influence the way we experience our lives.

CREATING POSITIVE PICTURES

Picturing Positive images →

At that point I decided to take charge of the "inner picture." Where there had been a dark, bleak picture of loneliness and helplessness, I began applying brush strokes in brighter, truer colors. In addition to drawing what I desired, I also practiced picturing things in my mind's eye the way I *wanted* them to be.

This approach even spilled over into my dream state. At night healers came to me in my dreams, bringing love and understanding. Powerful images of healing comforted me and gave me hope. Then the dream-pictures became a reality when my friends led me to gifted health practitioners who treated the whole person—body, mind, and spirit. One of these healers was a nurse trained in acupressure massage. Her treatments were very soothing and gave me the feeling of being understood and nourished. I felt better immediately.

After a few acupressure treatments I realized I needed help in dealing with the emotions that were coming to the surface: anger, resentment, and fear. I began seeing a psychotherapist who taught me, through Gestalt techniques, how to "dialogue" with the various parts of my life. I enacted confrontations with physicians who had misdiagnosed and over-medicated me during my illness. I also acknowledged my own fears and grief, and realized I had felt like an abandoned, orphaned child during the years of upheaval leading up to my illness. I had completely sup-pressed that frightened and sad inner child while trying to survive as a "responsible adult." My therapist gave me tools for nurturing and pro-tecting that inner child. She also referred me to a physician who treated me with great sensitivity and compassion. I immediately felt confident under this doctor's care as she took emotional and lifestyle factors into account.

Along with a few close personal friends, these professionals provided a much-needed support system. I now had new experiences that nullified my old beliefs. I was no longer alone—people were there for me after all. I developed a new "family," and one which I had chosen. My feelings of isolation and abandonment began to fade. A new strength, a healing power was emerging from within, and the physical symptoms started dis-appearing. The chronic fatigue lifted and my energy started coming back. The insomnia vanished and I began to feel rested and restored.

As I contemplated going back to work, it became clear that my old career as an artist and educator no longer had meaning for me. Friends with whom I had shared my journal urged me to explore the field of art therapy. In this approach the individual creates spontaneous art from the unconscious and, with the help of the therapist, interprets the deeper meaning of the forms and symbols that emerge. It is much like dream in-terpretation, except the dream is in the art. A new career was born!

Feeling nurtured by friends and health practitioners who reached out to me with love and compassion, I experienced life in a new way. Positive, life-affirming beliefs and images were filling my mind and feeding my heart. A new inner picture in which I was loved, supported, and cared for was replacing the old image of loneliness, fear, and isolation.

Drawing negatives into positives!

These new pictures and beliefs not only resulted in my complete physical recovery, but also gave me the courage to embark upon a new career. Whenever fears and doubts came up, I drew them out on paper and then created the image of how I wanted them to be. I had become the conscious gardener of my own mind. *I saw that I had choices*. This was one of the most profound and transforming realizations of my entire life:

I can decide which thoughts to cultivate.
I can believe whatever I choose to believe.
I can picture my life and myself the way I want them to be.

GOSSAMER FLUTTERINGS
DREAMS WINGING.
HUMMING TO MYSELF HIGHEST
FROM TIME REMEMBERED
FADING INTO NOW.

After my full recovery I drew this self-portrait showing how I felt about myself. Like a butterfly emerging from its cocoon, I was reborn into a life filled with new possibilities.

Now it is time to turn the drawing you did in "Body Picturing" into a positive image of health.

YOUR OWN PICTURE OF HEALTH

Purpose: Creating the image of how you want your body to feel; writing positive affirmations.

Materials: Your drawing from the "Body Picturing" exercise, colored felt pens, paper.

Look at the drawing you did for the "Body Picturing" exercise. Using your nondominant hand, create a new drawing of your body on a separate piece of paper that shows how you would like to feel. As you draw, imagine the feelings of health and vitality associated with your new picture. Label this picture "Health."

Around your picture create "word balloons" like those shown in comic strips. In each balloon allow your "Picture of Health" to speak about how it feels.

When Carole did the "Body Picturing" exercise in Chapter 3, her sinuses were stuffed up and her body ached. She described her symptoms as a cross between the Blues and the Blahs—the "Bluhhhhs."

Carole then drew her own Picture of Health and then did a visual affirmation entitled "Feeling Good and Getting Better."

Feeling Good and Getting Better

Matthew did the "Body Picturing" exercise in Chapter 3 and got in touch with blocked areas in his body.

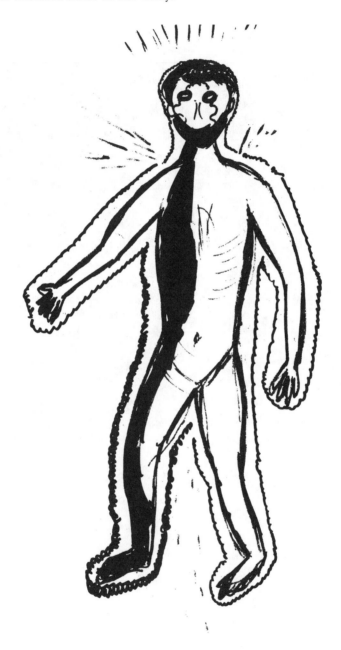

Matthew's Picture of Health shows his body clear of blockages and an open heart with energy flowing up his spinal column.

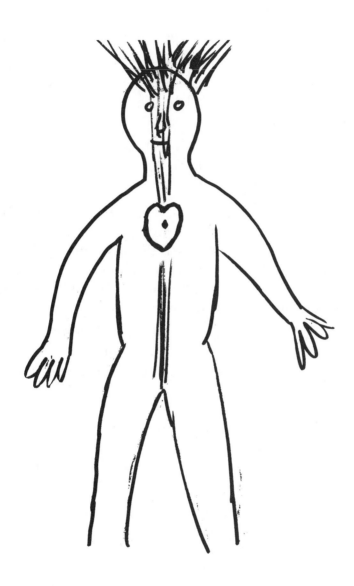

HERE'S LOOKING AT YOU, KID

Purpose: Developing the habit of creative thinking through mental imagery; reinforcing the image of your healthy self.

Materials: Your "Picture of Health" from the previous exercise.

Display your picture someplace in your home or work environment where you can look at it frequently. Consider it a visual affirmation, a portrait of how you wish to look and feel. Look at it as often as possible and read the words and phrases written on it.

After looking at your picture for a while, if you feel that it no longer accurately portrays the Picture of Health you wish to embody, redraw it. You can do this as often as you wish.

Develop the habit of remembering your Picture of Health and visualizing it in your imagination. Reinforce the picture by repeating the key words or phrases in your mind, using them as silent health affirmations. These affirmations are especially powerful and alive because they come from your own Inner Self. It is also important to integrate these affirmations into your daily speech whenever possible.

As you continue reinforcing this blueprint for health through your eyes, through your visual imagination, and through your words, notice signs of this picture becoming physical reality. Observe yourself living out the Picture of Health.

TALKING PICTURES

Purpose: Creating affirmations from your Picture of Health in order to reinforce your new image and make it a physical reality.

Materials: Your "Picture of Health," colored felt pens, paper.

Take your Picture of Health and study it for several minutes.

Allow it to come alive. Imagine that it can talk. With your nondominant hand allow the person in your picture to write a description of how he or she feels. Write it in the first person. For instance: "I feel so alive and full of energy. I am grounded and supported. I am bursting with life."

Let the picture continue talking through your nondominant hand. Let the person in the drawing write about how he or she became the Picture of Health.

Write positive affirmations to reinforce your Picture of Health.

Talking Pictures

I feel so Good!

LIFE IS SO SIMPLE!

LIVE YOUR TRUTH
AND STAND YOUR GROUND.
LET IT FLOW Through
YOU. LET LIFE
DO ITS DANCE
THROUGH YOU.
SURRENDER TO THE

Talking Pictures

TRUTH WITHIN!
IT HAS ALL BEEN
GIVEN TO YOU
ALREADY! THERE
IS NOTHING TO SEEK
BUT YOUR OWN
HEART!

Talking Pictures

CREATING A NEW BODY IMAGE

One of the most amazing phenomena I have discovered since recovering from the collagen disease is the plasticity of the human body and its ability to change. I first became aware of this when my friend Jane was being rolfed. Rolfing, or structural integration, is a form of deep tissue bodywork which helps to release old traumas and chronic tension patterns stored in the body.

At weekly lunches with my friend Jane, I noticed that she seemed taller, more vital and energetic. At the time she was in her mid-forties and had borne ten children. Although I attributed her change in appearance to weight loss, Jane informed me that it was due to rolfing. After a few more weeks, her posture and overall appearance were transformed so dramatically that I became intrigued and signed up for a series of ten sessions.

Since childhood I had held a body image of being awkward. I had repeatedly been told that I was clumsy, and because of the heart murmur I was not permitted to engage in sports or any "strenuous" childhood games. My secret desire was to be a dancer, and I wept bitterly when my parents informed me that I could not take ballet classes.

So the prospect of a new body image and the chance to experience physical grace and freedom was irresistible. After completing the series of ten rolfing sessions, I felt I had a new body that could do things it had never done before. I also had the confidence to try things I would never have attempted in the past. At age thirty-nine, my childhood dream came true when I began studying dance. At the same time, I revived an early love of roller skating (one of the few activities I had been allowed as a youngster) and also discovered, of all things, skateboarding.

The Playful Child in me had been liberated from the prison of my own mental restrictions. Enjoying my newfound freedom and physical agility, I noticed that pounds were dropping away with no effort and no dieting. It seemed like magic. The secret was in enjoying my body. It was like learning to walk and run for the first time. Each day was filled with new self-discoveries.

The changes in my appearance and attitude were also reflected in the new way that I dressed and "put myself together." Treating myself to silk clothes and flowing fabrics was a further expression of my new unrestricted and playful spirit. It was a time of self-nurturing and reviving a part of myself that had been dormant for years.

Since that time, I have encountered many individuals who have also experienced physical transformations from the inside out. Following are two stories which demonstrate the power of the mind and the emotions to "shape" the physical form in which we live.

My friend Mona Brookes is a well-known art educator and author of the best-selling book, *Drawing with Children*. As an artist she has extensive experience with the power of visual imaging. What is unique about Mona is that she has applied the "art" of visualization to her own self-image with great success. Although Mona is a slender and gracefully attractive woman, she told me that many years ago she was quite heavy and held a body image of being fat and awkward. She is now very agile and performs improvisational dance.

When I inquired about the changes in her body image and physical appearance, she smiled and answered, "I did it with my mind." She went on to tell me that she lost weight by picturing herself as graceful and slender.

Elizabeth Johnson's story is another dramatic example of the physical changes that can take place with the techniques presented in this book. She attended my creative journal seminar and soon became an enthusiastic and dedicated journal-keeper. Elizabeth experienced many benefits using these techniques, but the most visible was a weight loss of thirty-five pounds.

When I met Elizabeth in 1980, she was looking for a new career direction and seeking tools for personal growth and creativity. She enrolled in my weekly journal classes, and after a few months I noticed that she was becoming noticeably more slender. When I asked her how this came about, she explained that she was dealing with a weight problem in her journal work.

Elizabeth was exploring the emotional roots and implications of carrying extra weight. At the same time she was also creating a new picture of herself through drawings, collages, and journaling. Although she had struggled through numerous diets in the past, the weight was now dropping and staying off. Today, Elizabeth looks like a different person. She is slender and athletic and enjoys dancing. She no longer hides her bright light behind extra pounds and loose-fitting clothes. It is no accident that as Elizabeth came out of hiding, she revealed herself as a fine writer. In fact, we wrote a book together called *The Lighten-Up Journal: Making Friends with Your Body.*

A NEW YOU

Purpose: Changing your self-image; improving your body image.

Materials: Paper and assorted felt pens or colored pastels.

Draw a picture of your body as you imagine it in your own mind. Use your dominant hand to do this drawing.

Study your drawing carefully. Observe posture, appearance, and attitude. If you are not satisfied with the body image you drew, create a new picture of the image you would like to have of yourself. Do this drawing with your nondominant hand.

Place the picture of "the new you" in a spot where you can see it frequently. If your body image changes after you have looked at this drawing for a while, feel free to create a new picture. Repeatedly looking at the picture of the new you is a way of practicing visual affirmations and reinforcing a more positive image of yourself.

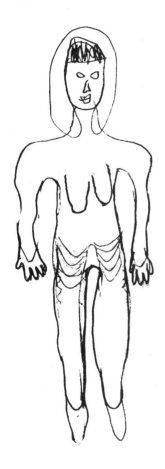

How I See Myself

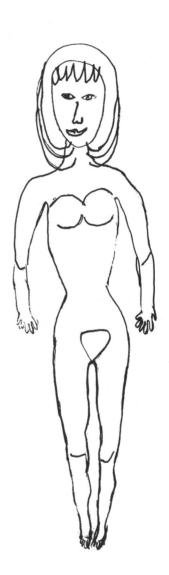

How I Would Like to See Myself:
"The New Me"

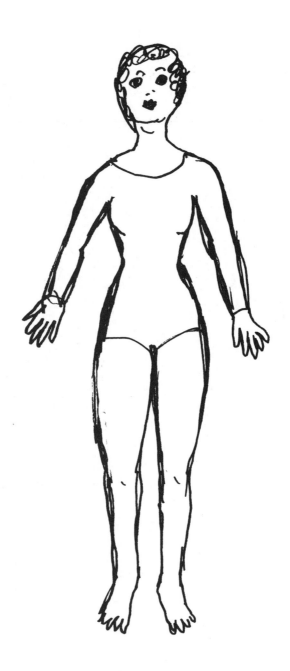

The Old Me

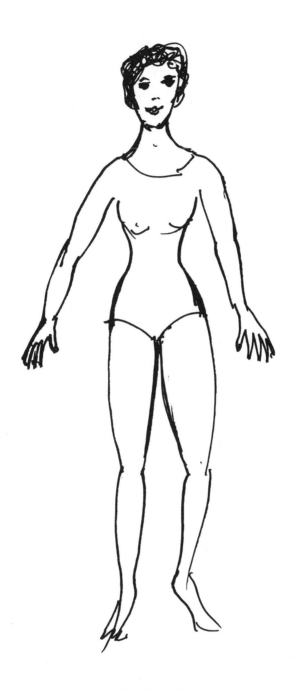

The New Me

A NEW YOU

After doing this exercise, the woman wrote out her observations about the two pictures, as follows:

In the first drawing I look heavy and immoveable. I am just standing there stiffly without much energy or vitality. My face even looks dull and lifeless.

In the second picture my body is light and more athletic. I have energy and look strong, ready for life, and ready to move. When I drew it I had much more conviction. My face is happy and shows confidence. When I look at this drawing, I think: I'd like to know this woman. She looks like fun.

MIRROR, MIRROR, ON THE WALL

Purpose: Changing negative perceptions of yourself.

Materials: Large mirror (preferably full-length).

Look at yourself in the mirror. See your reflection from the front, sides, and back.

Now look at yourself face-to-face. Focus on the features or qualities you like. Tell yourself something complimentary. For instance, "My hair is beautiful and healthy," or "I have a great smile." Do this as often as you can, and speak these affirmations to yourself mentally, even when you are not in front of a mirror.

Look at yourself in the mirror and notice the parts of your appearance you do not like, the parts you criticize and judge. Drop your judgment for a moment and look at each of these parts with love and gratitude. Thank each part for how it functions in your life.

5

Turning Your Worries Around

Prior to my recovery from the collagen disease, I had no understanding of where thoughts and feelings came from and how they shaped my life. I just *had* thoughts and feelings. Some were pleasant and some were painful. I often felt they had control over me, especially in the case of negative thoughts and worries. They were like unwanted house guests, and I was too timid to ask them to leave. For instance, worries used to keep me up all night and give me headaches. The fear that resulted from worries could affect my bladder, upset my stomach, or nearly paralyze me.

After my recovery I realized that *worry is imagination used self-destructively*. It is self-fulfilling prophecy, a dreary forecast based on negative seed-thoughts and mental pictures: "As you sow, so shall you reap." Chronic worrying comes from a habit of creating worst-case scenarios. This contributes to unhappiness and poor health. *Chronic worrying is a cancer of the mind that eats away at our vitality and self-confidence.* It is an addiction to negative thinking.

In contrast, *creative thinking is imagination used self-constructively*. It comes from right understanding about how the mind works. It is rooted in the desire to create a more fulfilling life, and the belief that it is possible to do so. This requires the creation of positive goals. Most importantly, creative thinking strengthens feelings of worthiness and self-love, and the motivation to "go for it" in our lives.

Creative thinking does not mean that we overlook the "dark side" or camouflage negative beliefs with positive affirmations. Rather, creative thinking reveals negative beliefs *in order to change them*. Change is made by remaining focused on your visions and goals, and refusing to let worries take over and sabotage your personal dreams.

One way to stay focused on desired goals is to draw the vision of what you want. The power of imagery through art is that you take it in through your eyes. This multisensory reinforcement is a call to action. Unlike mental pictures which are relatively ephemeral and can easily vanish from one's mind and memory, an image on paper is a concrete and enduring reminder. It can be seen again and again, and used as a visual affirmation.

This chapter contains techniques for pinpointing and counteracting the destructive effects of negative thinking. You will evoke the spirit of the Inner Warrior by confronting and conquering the demon: worry. This includes recognizing the worrisome thoughts that you habitually reinforce through your speech. You will then learn how to change your speech in order to change your life.

WHAT'S WRONG WITH THIS PICTURE?

Purpose: Learning to identify the areas of your life that worry you; turning a negative situation around through positive picturing.

Materials: Crayons, felt pens, or pastels in assorted colors.

Draw a picture of any aspect of your life that you are worried about. There may be more than one, but choose only one at this time. It can be any area: body, relationship, job, home, finances. Do your drawing in any style you wish: abstract doodles, scribbles, shapes, images, or symbols. Label your picture when you are through.

Look at your picture. Ask yourself how you would *like* the situation to feel. How would you like to experience that area of your life? Then draw a new picture that portrays those feelings. Give your new picture a name.

I feel sick — clogged up.
Blood moving so slow,
almost still, thick - like
lava as it slowly moves
cooling and thickening,
sickening

Cholestral & Fat

It's like the tar pits

Sticky

STJUX UGH

Help Help Help

Drain is clogged

I am healthy,
energetic and vibrant.
My blood is clean and
moves swiftly through
my body.
I am happily exercising
every day.
I am heathfully thin
and I radiate with
the cleansing light that
flows through me.
I glow as I grow and
I don't say "you know"
My communication runs as clear
as my blood— Free from
contaminants.

THE HEALING POWER OF LAUGHTER

A merry heart doeth good like a medicine:
But a broken spirit drieth the bones.
—Book of Proverbs

I learned about the power of smiling and laughter at a conference where I sat next to the main speaker during lunch. He was a well-known Indian yoga master who embodied the archetype of a wise old man: white robe, long white hair and beard, and eyes that expressed deep love and compassion. I sensed that he was an extraordinary being. While seeming keenly aware of everything around him, he was constantly chuckling and smiling as if he knew a sublime secret. As people were introduced to him, I noticed that his state of joy was utterly contagious. I watched the faces of everyone he met transform from serious and timid to open and joyful. Even now, just recalling the experience brings a smile to my face.

The healing power of laughter and smiling has been documented in recent years in several excellent books. In *Anatomy of an Illness*, Norman Cousins tells the story of his recovery from a life-threatening illness. He laughed himself back to health by viewing old comedy films by the Marx Brothers and others.

Today it is becoming more common to hear health professionals talk about the therapeutic value of humor and laughter. There are now professional conferences on the healing power of laughter and play. Participants are taught to juggle, tell jokes and stories, and entertain through mime and role playing. In his book *Love, Medicine and Miracles*, Bernie Siegel, M.D., writes that "a sense of humor is an enormous asset." He goes on to say:

> Many times when I'm in a room with a "dying" patient we are laughing. Out in the hallway, the other staff members think that we are denying reality. We're simply still alive and still able to laugh.

Modern Taoist master Mantak Chia writes about the "Inner Smile" in his book, *Taoist Ways to Transform Stress into Vitality*:

> Many people operate their lives in anger, sadness, depression, fear, worry, and other kinds of negative energy. These types of energy are

bound to cause chronic disease and steal our major life force. . . . In ancient China, the Taoist Masters recognized the power of smiling energy. . . . Smiling to one's self is like basking in love, and love can repair and rejuvenate. . . . The Inner Smile directs smiling energy into our organs and glands which are so vital to life.

Over the years I have found that laughter and play have immense therapeutic value. Early on in my art therapy practice, I began offering creativity workshops which can best be described as play therapy for adults. In these workshops "grown-ups" were allowed to act like children. They finger-painted and worked with clay, played musical chairs, dressed up, and improvised their own dances and plays. The atmosphere was always charged with hilarious laughter and a spirit of adventure. The most common reaction from the participants was: "This workshop was so *healing.* I feel so much younger and more alive."

FROWN: A SMILE TURNED UPSIDE DOWN

Purpose: Observing how negative states of mind affect your face and body.

Materials: Paper, pens, and mirror.

Sit or stand in front of a mirror. Breathe deeply and relax. Look at your reflection in the mirror and focus your attention on your face.

Think of something you are worried about at this time in your life. At the top of your paper write down your worry.

Next allow this worry to bring a frown to your face. As you frown become aware of the sensations in your face and in your body. Look at your frowning reflection in the mirror. Observe everything that is happening to your face: the expression in your eyes, the creases, wrinkles, and tension.

Draw a simple sketch of your frowning face. It can be a caricature or a cartoon. Just draw an impression of the frown, i.e., a furrowed brow, a pouting mouth. Around the picture write words or phrases that describe how you felt while frowning.

Frown: A Smile Turned Upside Down

Frown: A Smile Turned Upside Down

SMILE: PUT ON A HAPPY FACE

Purpose: Observing how positive emotions affect the face and body.

Materials: Paper, pens, and mirror.

Once again stand or sit in front of a mirror. Think of someone or something that makes you happy. Then allow a big smile to light up your face. Close your eyes and enjoy smiling. As you smile observe the sensations in your body. How do you feel?

Look at your smiling face in the mirror. Observe everything that is happening to your face, paying particular attention to your eyes. Note your reaction to the smiling image in the mirror.

Now draw a simple picture of the mirror image of your smiling face. Around the picture, write words and phrases that describe how you felt while smiling.

Put on a Happy Face

Put on a Happy face

WHEN YOU'RE SMILING,
WHEN YOU'RE SMILING

In your everyday life, observe how often you smile. When you notice you are smiling at something or someone, ask yourself, "How do I feel right now?" Take a mental snapshot of that feeling. Notice how others respond to your smile.

In your interactions with other people, make a point of observing when other people smile at you. Notice if it is a half-hearted or a genuine smile. What feeling does this smile evoke in you? How do you feel about the other person at that moment?

Next time you feel agitated or stressed out, take a moment to think about something that makes you smile. With your smile, "switch on" the inner light that vitalizes your immune system and other physical functions. Observe any changes in your body, your emotions, or your mental outlook.

watch others' reactions to your smile

THE WARRIOR WITHIN

I have heard many say that positive thinking, visualizations, and affirmations are a form of denial or avoidance of the harsh realities of life. Nothing could be further from the truth when these techniques are understood and used properly. In fact, it takes a real warrior to confront worries and transform negative thoughts into life-giving ones.

When I use the term _warrior_, it is in the psychological sense of one who battles with his or her own destructive patterns and tendencies. Our "Inner Warrior" enables us to confront anything in our lives that blocks our creativity and growth. The qualities of the Inner Warrior are vigilance, discipline, and courage. It takes great strength to face the negative habits that cast shadows over our lives, keeping us from fulfilling our goals and dreams.

One individual who successfully battled with her inner "demons" was Rosina, a woman who attended many of my workshops. She had recently moved to Carmel, California, where she was working as a real estate broker. One day everything went sour. Difficulties with business associates, a lawsuit, and car problems brought her to a dead stop. Rosina began asking herself a lot of questions.

While talking on the phone with a friend, she heard herself say: "I'm living in one of the most beautiful places in the world and yet I'm really unhappy. And in the past I've lived in beautiful places and was unhappy. Sure, there were some fun times, but underneath it all there was self-doubt and depression. What is that all about?"

After hanging up the phone she went to the bathroom mirror and stared intently at her reflection. Talking to herself, she queried, "Why are you so depressed? You've lived in the most wonderful places. What is your depression about?"

Suddenly she saw an image of her mother superimposed over her own face in the mirror. She realized in that moment that this depressed way of being was her mother's way of living. Her mother's belief system had gone something like this: "Earth is hell, heaven is when you die. Life is serving and suffering."

In this moment of truth, Rosina shook her head and declared: "No, Mama, that's you. That's not me. That's not who I am! Every time I feel this depression coming on I am going to face you in the mirror and say no!"

Rosina reported to me that she has been true to her promise. When she confronts her "depressed mother" in the mirror, she feels that she is exercising free choice: to live the way her mother lived or to accept and celebrate her own life and her own changes. As she continued to do this exercise and to seek the help of positive and supportive people, her self-image greatly improved. When she falls into self-doubt she asks herself, "Are you going to be Mama, or are you going to live your own life, Rosina?"

We each have our own hit parade of useless worries. Some worries are short-lived and others are chronic. The next exercise can help you dissolve your needless worries and gain your inner power by taking charge of your thoughts through positive imagemaking.

FROM WORRIER TO WARRIOR

Purpose: Acquiring tools for doing hand-to-hand combat with habitual worries, fears, and anxieties.

Materials: Paper and felt pens.

Draw a picture of yourself worrying. Around the picture write down your "top ten" worries about your life: your health, appearance, finances, work, relationships, etc.

Select number one on your hit parade of current worries. Allow an image of this worry to form in your mind. It might appear as a dark cloud, a dragon, a menacing shark, or an annoying fly. Draw a picture of the worry.

Now draw a picture of yourself disposing of the worry. Use whatever weapon or magic tool you wish—a sword, a laser gun, a broom, an ax, a fly swatter—to "dissolve" the worry.

Then, draw a picture of how you feel being victorious over your worry. Display this picture where you can see it often. Recall this picture to your mind whenever the worry returns.

From Worrier to Warrior

Ill never fully regain the use of my upper body.

My BACK WILL GET progressively worse.

Im becoming STIFF – immobile.

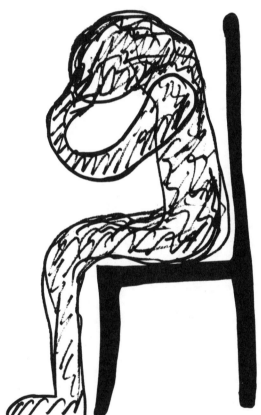

My Body IS Growing older & weaker.

I HAVE A real problem with my digestion.

Ill Never be able to be athletically active AGAIN.

My eyesight is Getting weaker.

My energy level will continue to drop.

Im slowly deteriorating.

I CAN NO longer RUN without hurting myself.

The Worrier

Confronting of Worries

From Worrier to Warrior

Freedom From Worry

The Worrier

Exhausted From Worry

Transforming Worry Through Love

A Worry-free Me

THE HEALING OF A WOUNDED WARRIOR

Thinking in mythological terms helps to put you in accord with the inevitables of this vale of tears. You learn to recognize the positive values in what appear to be the negative moments and aspects of your life. The big question is whether you are going to be able to say a hearty yes to your adventure . . . the adventure of the hero—the adventure of being alive.

—Joseph Campbell
The Power of Myth

I was privileged to meet a man whose fascinating story of healing integrates much of the philosophy and many of the techniques contained in this chapter. At age thirty-eight, Ben Hedges developed a lump in his groin and was diagnosed with Hodgkin's disease, a form of lymph cancer. The news came as a shock because Ben considered himself the "picture of health." A happily married man with three children and four jobs, he lived an extremely full and active life. As a marriage, family, and child counselor, he practiced psychotherapy and was also director of the expressive arts therapy department at John F. Kennedy University in the San Francisco Bay Area. His professional activities also included teaching and facilitating expressive arts programs at a residential adolescent treatment center. Expressive arts therapy is an approach to counseling in which visual arts, drama, poetry, storytelling, dance, and ritual are used in the service of personal growth. As with art therapy, the emphasis is on process, not product.

Ben was an avid athlete who worked out at the gym three times a week and ran 10K's in his spare time. He neither smoked, drank, nor ate red meat. He got a perfect score on any health assessment test he took. He does remember, however, that for some time before his diagnosis, he thought and actually said many times, "If I had only a year to live, I'd drop everything and go into the expressive arts for myself."

Following his diagnosis at a local hospital, Ben went to the Stanford University Medical Center where he was advised to undergo a laparotomy (a diagnostic surgery) and a spleenectomy. He had a lot of misgivings and decided to seek another opinion. He found an oncologist who bridged traditional medicine with holistic healing. This oncologist encouraged Ben to express his anger and fear of doctors and surgical techniques.

Ben told the oncologist that he felt like taking a sword or a weapon into surgery with him. The doctor said, "Yes, engage that warrior part of yourself." Ben also shared these thoughts with his friends at the university. They too supported his approach and gave him raw materials for making a "power object." Such symbolic objects and totems have been used by all cultures for protection. Native American medicine men or shamans used animal masks, costumes, and rattles as part of their healing rituals. One can also see vestiges of this use of symbolic objects in the ancient emblem of the medical profession, the caduceus—two serpents intertwined on a staff. This symbol represents the forces of healing and regeneration in nature. Using stone, jewelry, paper, and other materials, Ben fashioned a tomahawk/totem which he carried into the Stanford Medical Center when he arrived for surgery. He reported that it made him feel much stronger and brought a feeling of levity and outrageousness to the somber atmosphere normally surrounding surgical procedures.

After surgery Ben's body was scarred and he felt a great deal of anger and fear. He told the oncologist he felt medically invaded. The doctor reframed the situation by citing the "fighter" or "warrior" archetype and discussing the battle scars of heroes past. In traditional cultures shamans or healers were initiated through major tests of survival. These ordeals, or rites of passage, invariably included wounding and healing. It was through this firsthand experience of healing that the individual earned his role as healer in the society. This perspective, which also coincides with Jung's description of the "hero's journey" and the "wounded healer," resonated strongly within Ben since he was a therapist.

In five months of radiation therapy following the surgery, Ben wore various costumes and carried props to his treatments as a ritual protection. For instance, one day he wore a long black wig and a suit of armor into the hospital waiting room and down the halls to the treatment room. Although he could not wear his costume during the treatment, he felt protected from the damaging effects of radiation. And the technicians got a big laugh out of it.

During his radiation sessions, Ben also used visualization techniques that he had learned from the writings of Dr. Carl Simonton and Dr. Stephanie Matthews-Simonton, pioneers in the use of imagery with cancer patients. Ben used mental images of strength and protection.

In looking back on his hero's journey through diagnosis, surgery, and radiation, Ben felt that the work with his oncologist had provided the foundation for healing. This doctor had helped him give voice to his anger in the form of his warrior energy. He was even able to act out his anger through a playful wrestling match with the doctor. By expressing anger and humor, fear and fantasy, Ben was able to ritualize and "reframe" his entire experience from one of victimization to one of heroic empowerment.

Against all medical odds, Ben and his wife conceived and gave birth to a healthy baby during his healing journey. Out of confrontation with a life-threatening disease, Ben found a new inner life and helped to create life for a new human being. Today Ben is healthy, happy, and leading a productive and balanced life.

I have used many similar techniques such as mask making, sculpting in clay and other media, as well as dance and rituals for healing. In my experience, the expressive arts therapies are a particularly powerful form of healing because they reach far deeper into the unconscious mind where the psychological roots of disease are hidden.

Doing Battle With Cancer

The Victorious Warrior

THINK BEFORE YOU SPEAK

We shape our language and our language, in turn, shapes us.
—Marshall McLuhan

You have learned how to change negative pictures in your mind by identifying your worries through drawing and then creating a new positive image on paper. But gloomy forecasts come in the form of *words* as well. Almost everyone fosters negative thinking through bad speech habits. How many times have you heard (or said) things like:

> *"I always look terrible."*
> *"My relationships never work out."*
> *"Money is always tight."*
> *"I can never say no to food."*
> *"I always have boring jobs."*
> *"I have a bad back."*
> *"My car is always in the shop."*

Negative speech comes from negative thinking. However, we have it within our power to monitor our minds and discipline our thoughts the way we would an unruly child. When a child's behavior becomes unmanageable and destructive it is time for setting limits. The same thing applies to a worrisome mind. It can run wild and wreak havoc in our lives, so we need to achieve mastery over our thoughts.

One person who successfully transformed his addiction to worry and negative speech is David. Although he was a highly competent engineer, David constantly referred to himself in self-deprecating terms such as, "I am such an idiot," "With my bad luck," and "You cannot win." With this running monologue he reinforced his low self-esteem and projected an unattractive image to the world. No matter how much he accomplished professionally, he felt worthless. David's negative speech also pushed other people away and he found himself isolated much of the time. Nobody wants to be around people who are always putting themselves down and expecting the worst. His negativity became a self-fulfilling prophecy.

Fortunately, David grew weary of the negative results he was creating in his life, and this motivated him to seek help. In therapy he realized his own negative thoughts and attitudes were attracting undesirable situations to him. Through art therapy David worked on his self-esteem issues and began discovering his own self-worth. Then he began to witness his habitual worries and transform them into positive thoughts and statements.

One day we both had a good laugh in a therapy session when David started voicing a continuous train of worries. He caught himself in mid-sentence and waved his hand as though he were erasing the words he had just uttered. "Cancel those thoughts," he declared. Then he went on to restate his thoughts in a positive manner. After several weeks I observed a great change in David's attitude about himself. And best of all, David reported that he was feeling better than he had in his entire life. He realized that he had a good mind, but he had been using it destructively in his personal life. He actually began enjoying the practice of monitoring his thoughts so that they did not become negative.

Another person who retrained his mind through creative thinking is Ed, a well-known author and teacher of writing. As a professional writer, Ed was perfectly aware of the power of words. However, he had not realized how his body was being affected by his habit of negative speech. After reading my book, *The Power of Your Other Hand*, Ed started using my dialogue techniques for dealing with chronic stomach pain. One day he phoned me excitedly, telling me how relieved he had felt after doing the dialogues.

Then he told me: "Since I was a teenager, I have had a bad stomach." Suddenly, he stopped himself. "Listen to me," he exclaimed. "Listen to how I am talking about my stomach. No wonder it hasn't felt well. I have been thinking about it as *bad* and calling it *bad* for thirty years or more. I guess I better stop that right now." At that moment Ed became aware of how his words were influencing his physical health.

Practicing creative thinking and positive speech involves more than disciplining one's own mind and language. Sometimes we must be vigilant

Note

Other's negative speech —

✳

in monitoring the negative speech of others in our immediate environment. This does not mean that we tell others what to say or in any way try to change or criticize people around us. However, we can choose what to listen to, and we can tell others how their negative speech affects us.

Rosina had dramatic results with monitoring negative speech in a life or death situation. At the time, she was facing the "probable" death of her teenage daughter, Mary Jean, who was diagnosed with a brain tumor. The doctors and nurses offered virtually no hope for survival. But Mary Jean wanted to live, and Rosina stayed by her side to support her. One way she supported Mary Jean was by monitoring any fatal prophecies made by anyone within earshot of her or her daughter. If hospital staff or visitors made negative comments about Mary Jean's chances of survival, Rosina would either ask them to leave the room or keep their comments to themselves. Mary Jean is alive and well today, embarking on a career as a counselor to families dealing with serious or life-threatening illness.

Your negative beliefs have a life of their own. They are like a raging fire that is ignited by a single match but ends up devouring an entire forest. A destructive belief may be implanted in your mind with one simple statement. As that negative statement continues to be repeated and reinforced, the destructive belief becomes empowered. Over time this can have far-reaching effects on your physical and emotional health.

WHAT YOU SAY IS WHAT YOU GET

Purpose: Identifying the negative statements you make about your health or your life; transforming them into life-affirming statements.

Materials: Paper and felt pens.

On the left side of your paper list any negative statements you frequently make about yourself or your life. For instance:

> *"I never have enough money."*
> *"I will never lose this extra ten pounds."*
> *"My family drives me crazy."*
> *"I do all the work and get no credit."*

Instead of describing what you *do not want*, you will now describe (and eventually create) what you *do want*. Next to the negative beliefs you listed, rewrite each one so that it clearly states what you *do want*. For instance:

"I never have enough money." "I always have whatever I need."

Now draw a picture for each of your new positive beliefs. Caption each picture with the positive statement or affirmation.

Each day observe what you say about your life and your health. When you hear yourself saying something negative, stop and think about the belief that your words express. Ask yourself if you want to *reinforce* the belief, or if you want to *change* it. If you decide to change it, *speak* your new belief.

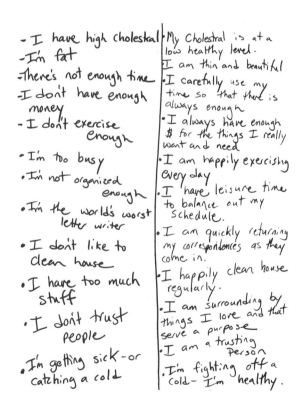

What You Say Is What You Get

6

Inner Healer, Inner Child

There is a child still living within all of us. It will never grow up and go away. This Inner Child is our emotional self; it is the seat of playfulness and creativity; and it is closely linked to our life-force energy and the essence of who we really are. The Inner Child has been described by many well-known psychologists, including Hugh Missildine, Eric Berne, Charles Whitfield, as well as Hal Stone and Sidra Winkelman. For a very fine, in-depth definition of the many aspects of the Inner Child, see the Stone and Winkelman books, *Embracing Our Selves* and *Embracing Each Other*.

Our Inner Child still carries emotional wounds from childhood—the fears, the anger, the sadness we were forbidden to express. It takes great inner strength to look at those vulnerable parts of yourself that are in need of healing. But in order to be healed they must be recognized and embraced. Much of the strength required for healing the Inner Child will come as a result of developing your Inner Warrior. Your commitment to training your mind to think creatively makes it safe for your Inner Child to come forth.

Positive speech and visual affirmations will be rewarded with increased self-confidence (as you have discovered in previous exercises). The practice of reshaping your thoughts, pictures, and words to match your desired results is empowering. Once you have expended the effort to discipline your unruly mind, a magical grace begins to fill your life. You are ready to form a true partnership with your Inner Healer, that universal, unlimited spirit or Higher Power that we all carry inside.

After many years of practicing creative thinking, positive speech, and visual affirmations with great satisfaction, I began meditating daily under the guidance of a meditation master. The more I meditated the more I became aware of the wounded child within myself. I would start crying for no apparent reason or feel a deep sense of grief without understanding why. In retrospect I can see that it had become safer for my wounded child to come out—because I had curbed the critical mind that used to berate her mercilessly for feeling vulnerable or frightened. I had been programmed to be strong, grow up, and stop all those weak "childish feelings." But now I was giving myself permission to let tears flow even when I was not sure why I was crying. (It was usually old grief from past experiences that I had accumulated.)

One day while I was attending a weekend workshop conducted by my meditation teacher, Gurumayi Chidvilasananda, I experienced a profound healing. While sitting in meditation with my eyes closed, I began crying. Years of bottled-up grief came spilling out. The longer I cried, the younger and more vulnerable I felt. Suddenly I saw a mental picture of myself carrying a helpless infant in my arms. Then in my mind's eye the image of my Inner Healer appeared. I approached her with great relief and offered the wounded infant into her loving embrace. As I did this, I felt showered with grace from a Higher Power within myself. I was being healed from an unlimited source of compassion and love, far beyond my own individual efforts. And yet the healing all happened within my own heart.

This chapter will help you discover your own Inner Healer, begin to heal the wounds of the child within you, and allow yourself to be more playful.

DRAWING OUT YOUR INNER HEALER

Purpose: Contacting your Inner Healer; creating a pictorial image to use as a visual affirmation of your own healing power.

Materials: Paper, felt pens, or pastels in assorted colors.

Take a moment to contemplate your Inner Healer. Now, using your nondominant hand, allow your Inner Healer to draw a picture of itself.

Now, have a written dialogue with your Inner Healer. You will speak with your dominant hand and the Inner Healer will speak through your nondominant hand. Use a different color for each hand. Ask questions about anything in your body or your life that needs healing. Let the Inner Healer guide you.

In this drawing, the Inner Healer appears as two infinity symbols, a vital energy representing unlimited possibilities. The artist showed herself asking for guidance in the scribbled form on the lower right.

Sarah, whose body drawing and dialogue appear in Chapter 3, did the following dialogue with her Inner Healer in the same workshop. When she shared her work with the group, Sarah became teary-eyed and was visibly moved by the guidance she received.

DIALOGUE WITH INNER HEALER

SARAH'S DIALOGUE

R: Inner Healer, please talk to me and tell me how I can be healed. What do I need to do?

L: Don't let others take away your time alone. Banish those who criticize—for you hold the keys to our kingdom.

R: Am I on the right path?

L: You are always learning the next lesson.

R: What should I do to still the voice of fear and anger?

L: Meet each challenge. As you turn to face the bullies, they will melt.

R: How can I get rid of old memories that are no longer a part of my life but still hurt?

L: Talk to each of them—one at a time—and see why they are still with you.

R: What else do I need to know?

L: The child within is the perfect rose. Watch it as the bud becomes a flower and each petal unfolds. Cherish it. Feed and nurture it and glory in its beauty.

Sarah's drawing shows the expansiveness and welcoming embrace of her Inner Healer.

Sue Maxwell, an American artist and writer living in Japan, corresponded with me while reading my book, *The Power of Your Other Hand.* She sent me this picture and poem from her Inner Healer, which she had created with her nondominant hand.

I am your healing -
heart, hands, eyes,
love - joy is yours to
give to all who come

Look on me and know
your healing and give

thanks to your Maker
and Healer, the giver
and source of all
life. He is life + to
know Him is life
    eternal.

Sue also wrote a dialogue with her Inner Healer using both hands. As you will notice in the following example, her Inner Child is the focus of the healing.

ANOTHER DIALOGUE WITH THE INNER HEALER

SUE'S DIALOGUE

R: Who are you? I sense you trying to emerge.
L: I am your beautiful grown self, tall, willowy, graceful, flowing vibrant, gentle, firm, resolute, in control, confident.
R: What is stopping you?
L: Your child who was never pampered, held, cuddled, loved, needed, taught, and who never let them know how much she hurt.
R: What can I do to help?
 L: You can love your child. Don't expect John (your husband) to. That's not his job. His job is to love you.

In dialoguing with her Inner Healer, Sue learned that she was responsible for loving and nurturing her Inner Child. No one could do it for her. This knowledge—that only we can take care of our Inner Child—is essential for health and healing.

HEALING THE INNER CHILD

The Inner Child knows what it knows through feelings, sensing, and intuition. It is often nonverbal like a very small child. If it is not acknowledged, it may seek attention through illness, accident-proneness, low energy, and destructive "acting out." This is the vulnerable aspect of the Inner Child speaking through the body. I will refer to it as the Vulnerable Child.

At the Los Angeles Center for Living, where I have conducted workshops on healing the Inner Child, it is openly acknowledged that there is a child still present in every adult. The L.A. Center, founded by Marianne Williamson, provides support groups and counseling for people with life-threatening and chronic illness: including AIDS, cancer, and Chronic

Fatigue Syndrome. Helping individuals attend to the frightened, Vulnerable Child within has been an important aspect of the services offered there.

Upon first visiting the L.A. Center, I was struck by its beauty; it is a lovely home decorated in soft colors, looking out onto a lush fern garden and pool. In the kitchen and dining room, food was being prepared and served. The nurturing atmosphere was far from the impersonal, clinical settings where most medical treatment takes place.

My own Inner Child felt immediately at home there. I also noticed that there were stuffed animals everywhere, clustered about on the sofas in all three meeting rooms. When I asked if children were being treated there too, my host smiled and replied, "Well, yes, we treat the inner children of the adults who come here for counseling and support." The L.A. Center for Living is truly a model environment for healing. I feel its effectiveness can be attributed to the fact that the Inner Child is recognized and revered there.

As part of your healing process, try to be aware of your environment; is your home a place where your Inner Child feels welcome and safe?

NURTURING YOUR INNER CHILD

Purpose: Learning to listen to your Inner Child and discovering its needs and wants.

Materials: Paper, crayons, and felt pens.

Let your Inner Child draw a picture of itself. Do this drawing with your nondominant hand. In your picture include some of the people, things, places and activities that your Inner Child likes best.

Have a dialogue with your Inner Child and ask it how it feels and what it would like from you.

Ask yourself, "What favorite things or activities do I turn to when I need nurturing?" Let your Inner Child make a list of these nurturing things and activities. Print it with your nondominant hand.

Next time you need nurturing, try following your Inner Child's wishes and see how you feel.

The examples by Christina, Ben, and Sue that follow will help you envision this process.

this is how i feel sometimes — like i have no skin + no way to keepfrom being hurt and vulnerable · it hurts physically to be so open + yet there's a lot of me i can't let out or let show because it's too painful and scary

DIALOGUE WITH THE VULNERABLE CHILD

After making the preceding drawing, Christina wrote a dialogue that helped bring out the pain and frustration of her Vulnerable Child.

Christina's Dialogue

CHILD: (LEFT HAND)   this is how i feel sometimes—like i have no skin & no way to keep from being hurt and vulnerable. it hurts physically to be so open & yet there's a lot of me i can't let out or let show because it's too painful and scary

CHRISTINA: (RIGHT HAND)   What do you feel you can't show?

CHILD: feelings, emotion—like when i try to sing with emotion all i can do is cry. and if i play music from my heart i cry. if i am in front of other people i have to shut down a lot in order to perform & be normal. if i paint realistically i am good at it but it bores me now. if i paint abstract i feel unqualified & like the art i'm doing is not very good. i also feel held back—i know there's a lot more to let out but i don't know how. i want to paint messy & free but if i do i usually feel like what i do is worth about 10¢ & it's meaningless to anyone else.

Children intuitively know the healing power of certain objects. A favorite blanket or teddy bear often brings comfort when nothing else works. For instance, they confide in their favorite dolls or stuffed creatures. This is demonstrated in the classic children's book, *The Velveteen Rabbit*, a story about a little boy's favorite stuffed animal. The Velveteen Rabbit became a *real* rabbit because the boy loved him so much.

In the photograph shown here, Ben Hedges, The Wounded Warrior from Chapter 5, cuddles a favorite stuffed animal. In the process of healing himself from cancer, Ben listened to his frightened Inner Child and responded with love and care. This is especially difficult for men to do, as there is so much societal pressure to be strong and "manly" at all times. Ben had the advantage of having been a wonderful parent to his own children before his bout with cancer. He knew what it meant to be a nurturing parent to them. Now he was able to turn that nurturing inward to his own frightened self.

* Think of the time your inner self saved you—comforted you—so to regain that trust in yourself.

In the following dialogue, Sue Maxwell received guidance from her Inner Healer about how to nurture her Vulnerable Child, Doe. She also learned of the woman within herself called Joy—a magical mother-healer figure. With poetic images of nature, Sue weaves a mythical story from her own rich inner world. She ends by discovering Doodles, her magical and playful Inner Child.

Sue's Dialogue

R: Do you have a name-child? Do you have a name-woman?
L: My child is Doe. A gentle fawn to love. You may make her a part of your adult self—integrate her gentle qualities. Play with her. The name of the woman is "not known." She has been veiled in mystery. But for now you may know the part of her called Joy. She has deep joy like a well. If you call on her she will come when you need her. She resides by a small pool of water in a woods and warms herself in

the afternoon sun. That is her mythological self. The other part of her—the mother part—wears a flowing red gown and comes as the mother-healer.

R: How can I heal the part of me that was never a mother—I've never had children?

L: You are a mother now. All women are mothers. First you will heal your own child Doe, by playing with her. Then play with other children and teach and heal them. Then your mother-healer—Joy—will emerge to teach and heal and love.

Sue's dialogue continued the next day:

R: Where does Doe live?

L: She hides in a protected area of a woods. She is very shy and vulnerable. She'll come out if you go to her.

R: How do I find her?

L: Go to the same place in yourself.

R: I don't know how—I've covered it over.

L: It's been a protected place for years. But it's beautiful. It's the woods and you love the woods.

R: I'm supposed to play with Doe?

L: Doe is very playful but she's never been allowed to play. She had to be so serious because life was so awful and difficult for her.

R: What does she want to play at?

L: Jump for joy. Do things just for the value and fun and enjoyment of doing them. Have fun—laugh—play games, make dolls, toys.

R: I'm too tired to play tonight—will you come and play with me tomorrow in my garden—and maybe go for a walk—I'll show you my favorite things.

L: Doe understands. You need rest tonight. But she can draw a picture of herself—and tell you her secret play name—it's "Doodles." Don't tell anyone—it's a secret play name—only given to special friends like you.

R: Thanks—It's a funny, cute name—you have a special sense of humor, I see.

L: You are surprised, aren't you? There's more to come—hang on.

Then Sue drew Doodles and went to bed. The next day, she spoke to Doodles:

R: Doodles, I think you look more like Doe and like you've been in the woods too long—kinda faded and neglected.

L: I am Doe—just her playful self. I'm tired of being by myself in the woods. I need to come out and have fun. That's why you've been buying all of those bright colored paper and Japanese toys lately— you can't keep me down any longer.

R: What do you like to play at—how about today, Doodles, this morning for a hour let's do something.

L: How about skipping down the street for joy and enjoy the feeling of our body and then walking along the beach barefooted.

R: I hope we have time—I'm going into Tokyo today—I guess I could do it now while it's early.

YOUR PLAYFUL CHILD

Purpose: Getting in touch with the playful part of yourself; learning
            to integrate play into all aspects of your life.

Materials: Large sheets of newsprint, magazines with color photo-
            graphs, scissors, glue, colored felt pens, and other drawing
            supplies of your choice.

Have a dialogue with your Playful Child, that spontaneous, fun-loving, adventurous spirit that lives within you. In this dialogue, ask your playful child how it would like to come out in your life at this time. How would it like to express itself in your work, your relationships, your home, your leisure time? Write the questions with your dominant hand; let your playful child answer with your nondominant hand. Use a different color pen in each hand.

In the center of another sheet of paper, draw a picture of your Playful Child. Leave space around the central image. If you have a photograph of yourself playing as a child, you may want to photocopy it and glue it in the center of the paper instead of drawing the image. Now take your magazines, and find photographs that show the kinds of people, places, things, and activities that your Playful Child likes. Then do a collage by gluing your photos onto the paper around your Playful Child image. Cut out appropriate words, phrases, and captions that you find in your maga-zines and glue them into your collage. With your nondominant hand, you can also invite your Inner Child to write meaningful words and phrases.

Display your picture in a place where you can see it regularly. Use it as a visual affirmation to reinforce this image of your Playful Child. Include some of your Playful Child's wishes into your life every day.

This drawing by Eve was done after she attended my Inner Child work-shop. By having continuing dialogues with her Inner Child, Eve felt a deep healing and a new sense of joy that are both expressed in this pic-ture. Her Playful Child did the collage that follows, showing all the things she likes.

My Inner Child

What My Playful Child Likes

In the following dialogue Christina contacted her Inner Child, Tina. This led to her creative Magical Child, who drew and wrote a lovely poem.

CHRISTINA'S DIALOGUE WITH TINA

TINA: i want to paint only from my heart and what i see inside. i have special secrets to share. please let me do that soon. and i want to draw ink pictures for rubber stamp making. Oh! we have lots to do and say, n'est pas? Let's have fun together. i want to sing and dance and play play play.

i want to do stuff that's only from me. listen to me let me talk. when i paint and draw like that i am so happy and my heart is full of love only and feelings that are good and i know you want that but you are hiding from me like a turtle. hey turtle come on out and play with me. it's lonely without me and you

CHRISTINA: What do you want to do first?

TINA: paint the night flower painting
find out about rubberstamp makers
i want to paint clothes too
i want to paint paint paint!
i am your magical child
my name is aurora
i am dancing with the stars
i am loving the universe
i am cherishing life and love
and the mysteries of the cosmos
i am flying to the mountain tops
i am praising the creator by
my dance and i am shouting
at the top of my lungs with joy
and rapture and wonder

i am created by love
and i give love
by dancing singing drawing
planting painting writing
dreaming
my heart is full of love
my mind is free to imagine all
that it can
my body is surrounded by light
there is only happiness in my
world
only love light and joy
and unlimited possibilities

tina
may 12, 1989

i am your magical child
my name is ayrora

"Aurora" went on to describe her vision of a new place to live.

> we need a special place to live
> i am dreaming of it for you
> i am visualizing a place that has loads of charm and
> atmosphere a fireplace lots of light and room to paint
> a sweet little kitchen
> place for planting herbs veggies and roses and sweet peas
> a place we can be loving and happy in

A few weeks later, Christina and her husband found a condominium with the same kind of doors and windows shown in Aurora's picture. Just as in the dialogue it had a fireplace, a charming kitchen, and a room for an art studio.

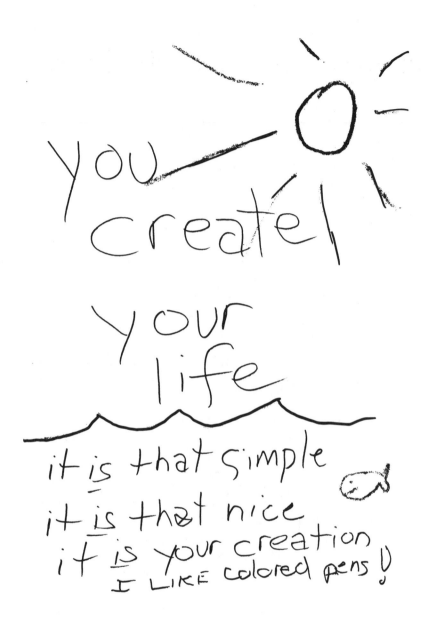

you create
your
life

it is that simple
it is that nice
it is your creation
I LIKE colored pens !

7

Blueprint for a Healthy Lifestyle

As you have celebrated the creative power within yourself using the techniques in this book, you have also been preparing to *create your life with awareness*. This is the time to integrate and apply all of the creative healing skills you have learned so far. This chapter is about consciously creating the lifestyle you want. Using the same process that playwrights and screenwriters employ, you will develop the visual script or storyboard for your life. You will become the producer, director, writer, as well as the actors in your own movie.

One way you will be integrating the many roles you play and the various aspects of your life will be to explore an ancient form of symbolic healing: the mandala. Through the creation of your own mandala, a circular design motif, you will visualize yourself becoming more centered in your own life. This will allow you to take charge of your dreams and visions, rather than feeling like a victim of circumstance. As you plant and cultivate the seeds of new visual images in your creative unconscious, your life will unfold naturally and gracefully like a flower.

When filmmakers are developing a new script, they make a "storyboard." A storyboard resembles the boxed cartoons featured in comic strips. A series of pictures tells a story with a caption underneath each picture or frame. Now you are about to make a storyboard for your Picture of Health.

MAKING YOUR OWN MOVIE

Purpose: Creating visual affirmations

Materials: Large sheets of unlined paper, colored felt pens or colored pencils.

Review the pictures and dialogues you have done with your body, your Inner Healer, and your Inner Child. What is the area of your life that most needs healing at this time?

Now, create a storyboard grid similar to comic strips, with boxes sequenced from left to right. In the first set of boxes, picture yourself doing the things that your "inner advisers" recommended for improving your health and the quality of your life.

Making Your Own Movie

These drawings can be very simple, with stick figures and rough sketches. In captions beneath the pictures or "word balloons" next to your figures, write out the activities and the feelings that result from these drawings. Write the captions in the first person singular, present tense, as positive affirmations. For example, the following can be captions under a series of drawings:

"I go to the gym on a regular basis."
"I enjoy riding my bike every day."
"I love sitting in the hot tub and sauna."

Display your storyboard in a place where you can see it and reinforce the images in your mind. *Make a point of writing these activities on your calendar, or in your appointment book so you don't forget them.*

Contemplate your storyboard and imagine doing the things illustrated there. In your mind visualize yourself doing the activities that you pictured. Imagine your body going through the movements of these activities. What do you feel? What do you see and hear? What physical sensations do you experience in each activity? This imagery will set your unconscious mind to work, helping you convert your "movie" into reality.

CENTERING THROUGH MANDALA ART

Making a mandala is a discipline for pulling all those scattered aspects of your life together, for finding a center and ordering yourself to it. You try to coordinate your circle with the universal circle.

—Joseph Campbell
The Power of Myth

The word *mandala* means "magic circle" in Sanskrit. The mandala is a circular design that has been used since ancient times to invoke the spirit of healing. Mandalas have appeared in many forms throughout history: in Tibetan meditation banners, the rose windows of Gothic cathedrals, and the Aztec calendar stone. In Navaho sand paintings, mandala designs are used for healing the sick. The goal is to bring the individual back into harmony with the cosmos. In the East, especially in Buddhism, mandalas are used as a focusing device for deepening meditation and contemplation.

Jung was responsible for bringing the mandala form into psychotherapy as an integrative and centering device. Through mandala art, individuals were encouraged to place a symbol for the Self at the center of the page. It is significant that the design unfolds from the center of the page as from the center of the Self. In his book *Mandala Symbolism*, Jung shared the case study of a client who had created mandalas over a period of years. In vivid color and exquisite design, we observe the artist's soul unfold before our very eyes.

I discovered mandala art when I was training to become an art therapist. It was a hectic time in which I was working to support myself, raising two small children, and carrying a full academic load. Fortunately, part of my graduate program included assignments in self-reflective art. I sat quietly each day and created a mandala in pastels, watercolors, and pencils. Those quiet art sessions were a shelter from the storm of my busy life. I experienced mandala making as visual meditation.

magic circle

The mandala is especially suited for visual representations of one's inner and outer worlds. The very structure of a mandala, with the design elements radiating out from the centerpoint, is intended to put you at the *center of your life*. For our purposes you will use the mandala as a tool for seeing a panoramic view of yourself, and for designing the blueprint of a healthy lifestyle. You will be using this ancient form of expression in creating the life you want today.

THE BIG PICTURE: PART ONE

MANDALA OF YOUR LIFE TODAY

Purpose: Learning to look at your life through creating mandalas.

Materials: Unlined paper, colored felt pens, pastels, crayons, or other drawing instruments of your choice. Other media such as watercolor and collage are optional.

Draw a border around your page. It can be any shape—oval, rectangular, square, or circular. In the center create an image that represents you. It might even be a photograph of yourself or a symbolic form with which you identify, such as a rose, a tree, or an animal.

Radiating out from your symbol in the center, create a circular design which portrays the most significant elements of your life as it is today. The following are some possible themes to include in your mandala:

Body	Health
Work	Relationships
Recreation	Personal growth
Creative expression	Spiritual practice

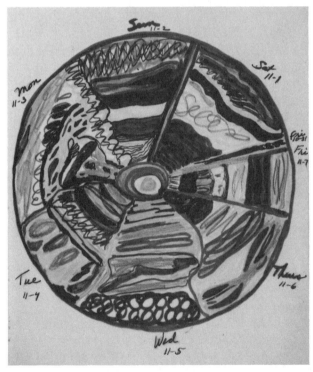

This mandala by Jane Murphy shows a week in her life. Each piece of the circle represents one day of the week and portrays her feelings through brightly colored abstract designs. The center of the mandala contains an eye looking out and observing her life.

In another mandala, done at a different time, Jane showed various aspects of life: "suffering" (outer ring); "understanding" (second ring); "letting be" (third ring); "peacefulness" (center).

THE BIG PICTURE: PART TWO

MANDALA OF A HEALTHY LIFESTYLE

Purpose: Drawing your life the way you want it to be.

Materials: Large sheets of unlined art paper, magazines or printed material with pictures and captions, personal photographs, scissors, glue, colored felt pens, and other art supplies of your choice (pastels, crayons, colored pencils, watercolors).

Draw a border around your page as you did in the last exercise. Again, it can be any shape—a circle, a rectangle, or a square.

At the center of your page place a symbol that represents your Inner Self, Higher Power, or God. You may want to use a photograph or design your own symbol.

Radiating out from the symbol at the center, create a mandala of your life the way you want it to be. Draw images or symbols, use photographs or captions from magazines, and write your own words in and around the mandala. Picture the important areas of your life as you would like to live them: relationships, home environment, work, play, and other activities.

When your mandala is complete, look at it for a while and then write your observations.

Place your mandala where you can see it on a regular basis. Use it as a visual affirmation that you can and will create the life you want, in the same way you have created the mandala: always centering at your source of strength and creativity, and radiating outward.

Make a new mandala from time to time to update your picture of a healthy lifestyle. It is a good idea to consult your body through written dialogues before doing a mandala. Ask it what it needs, and let your body express itself as you create your design.

Mandala of a Healthy Lifestyle

My Life As It Is Today

My Ideal Life:
Home is where my heart is; from it comes spiritual,
love, creativity, sharing, giving, etc.

The over all picture is dark — the emotional climate dominates every part of my day and everything I do. I am really a happy gentle soul but I am affected too heavily by the dark emotions. I would like to see more light, more sunshine in my life. The pink of my heart is even becoming dark; I would like the pink to be clear and bright and permeate every part of my being.

Take away the dark and replace it with more heart, more light and more spiritual lavender. Open the channels of communication — both within myself and outwards towards others. I know it is possible. How to actually do it? By doing what I am doing right now — working consciously on my self-esteem!

After doing a series of mandalas, Eve created one entitled "My Values." She wrote what each part of the mandala symbolized (she did the drawing and the writing with her nondominant hand):

> *My Values: The center radiating outward is my relationship with God, meditation, and service to God. The yellow flames are the circle of fire and represent protection and security, safety. The turquoise is appreciation and thankfulness. The orange petals are honesty and trust, shown through consistency. The red dots radiating outward and getting progressively larger are kindness, consideration, and love for others. The section at the bottom is being loving and supportive of others, i.e., family. The lines are reminders that everyone's path is a different color and shape. The turquoise demonstrates that some paths don't come together until later. (See inside back cover for a color rendition of Eve's mandala.)*

Some of the other elements that Eve included in her mandala of a healthy life are: productivity, efficiency, and the ability to create; financial independence, abundance, service to others (community and humanity), knowledge, intellectual growth, beauty, and aesthetics.

"My Values"
Mandala of a Healthy Life

YOUR PERSONAL POWER SYMBOL

Purpose: Creating a meaningful symbol for visualizing your inner
strength and protection in difficult situations.

Materials: Paper, felt pens, pastels, or crayons.

Ask your Inner Healer to reveal an image of your own personal power.
This image can come in the form of an animal, an object, an aspect of
nature, a person, or even a religious symbol—a cross, a Star of David, or
a depiction of an Om. It might be the symbol that you used in the center
of your mandala in the previous exercise.

Draw a picture of your personal power symbol. This is a symbol that pro-
tects you as well as gives you strength; be sure to portray the shielding,
protective aspect of the symbol. When you are in a difficult situation,
picture that symbol in your mind and feel the strength that it represents
for you.

You may want to develop a series of drawings showing the symbolic development of your own inner strength. Use these as meditation and
visualization images.

In this series of drawings by Jane Murphy, we see the development of a
symbol of personal strength and protection. Beginning with a meditation
drawing in which she found "a light in the cave," Jane went on to draw
the transformed flame as "Woman/Women in the Cave." The smaller
shape is a baby, contained by a larger one, representing the mother. These
two are encompassed by a number of larger forms that portray the Grand-
mother/Wise Woman archetype. In this way, Jane acknowledged the
power of the feminine principle in its many forms. Jane then drew a more
detailed version of the "light as a flame" by creating a brightly burning
lamp protected by a strong border. The last two abstract drawings show
the use of this symbol in Jane's everyday life. She encountered some
difficult situations that could have become what she called "self-esteem
downers." Instead, she owned her own power by visualizing her protected
inner light, and did not allow her self-esteem to be damaged in any way.

My Personal Symbol: A Light in the Cave

Woman/Women In the Cave   *Light As a Flame*

Protected Inner Light

8

With a Little Help
From My Friends

Friends can be good medicine.
        —Robert Ornstein and David Sobel
        The Healing Brain

Over the years I have learned that a personal support system is *absolutely essential* for achieving any kind of success and fulfillment. Whether one's personal goal is to recover from an illness, launch a more satisfying career, or learn new skills of any kind, support is necessary. When we are sick, we may call a doctor, or ask a neighbor to pick up something from the grocery store, or get a friend to drive our kids to school. When we have other kinds of needs, whether we are looking for a job, an apartment, or an accountant, we again expand our support system in order to meet our needs. Without a support system, we operate from a severe (and sometimes crippling) disadvantage. The myth of the rugged individualist who is totally self-made—an island unto himself—is a fiction, and a dangerous one at that. It misleads people into thinking they must face their crises alone. This is seen in the stereotype depicted in films and novels: the lone lawman in a western town or the hardnosed private detective are "heroic" in their stoic self-containment.

A healthy support system is composed of people we feel safe with, whom we can rely on, and whom we respect and support in return. Without such people around us, life can be an unnecessary struggle. The kind of support system I am referring to is one that we *choose consciously* because it meets our needs.

Contrary to American myth, our family members do not automatically qualify as a healthy support system simply by virtue of their relationship to, and history with, us. Unless they can encourage us in an uncontrolling and nonmanipulative way to be who we really are and to achieve our own goals, they do not qualify as an effective support system. For instance, one may receive financial assistance from a family member, but the strings attached may be so limiting that the "support" becomes a heavy burden.

You can create a new family for yourself, a family of friends and loved ones which may or may not include blood relatives or traditional family members. There are support systems of all kinds, informal and formal. For instance, your next-door neighbor may be part of your informal support system. You may meet spontaneously to share good news, commiserate in times of trouble, borrow a hammer, or get a ride to work when your car is in the shop. There may be other members of your support system, like out-of-town friends and family, with whom you only have telephone contact or written correspondence.

Support groups that meet on a regular basis are more formal by nature with an ongoing schedule, purpose, and structure. One of the best examples of a support system designed to meet specific needs—sobriety and recovery from addictive behavior—is the Twelve-Step program originated in Alcoholics Anonymous. In recent years we have seen the formation of many support groups for individuals with life-threatening illnesses or chronic pain, and for those who are recovering from loss. These groups function as an extended family of people experiencing the same difficulties. It is from this common ground that group members share their "experience, strength, and hope."

We look to members of our own personal support system to assist us in many different ways. For instance, when I need emotional support and understanding, there are several people in my life whom I know I can count on. They know how to listen to my feelings and how to simply be there for me. Just being able to talk out a problem with any one of these individuals is immensely therapeutic.

There are other individuals whom we seek out for their skills, knowledge, information, or contacts. In the field of career counseling the term "networking" is used to describe the skill of creating such a support system. This bears out the old adage, "It is not *what* you know, it is *who* you know."

If you are alive on the planet today, you already have a support system: water, food, oxygen, shelter, clothing, and the like. But beyond basic physical support, you have many other needs that you meet through myriad resources and people.

YOUR SUPPORT SYSTEM

Purpose: Identifying your support system; expressing appreciation to those who support you.

Materials: Paper and colored felt pens.

Make a list of all the people in your personal support system. These are people you turn to when you need help and encouragement, a sounding board, information, or a different perspective on things. As you make your list, ask yourself about the *quality* of support each person provides. Are they there for you when you need them? Are you there for them? Can you count on them in a crisis? Do they pressure you or put heavy expectations on you in return for their "help"? Do they want you to do things their way or do they trust your ability to know and meet your own needs? Do they respect you and allow you to be yourself?

Draw a picture of yourself surrounded by the primary members of your support system.

Write a note of thanks to each of the people in your picture, thanking them for their friendship, love, and support. In your note tell each person specifically what he or she has done for you and how it has affected your life.

Now, draw a picture of yourself feeling supported, loved, and accepted for yourself just the way you are.

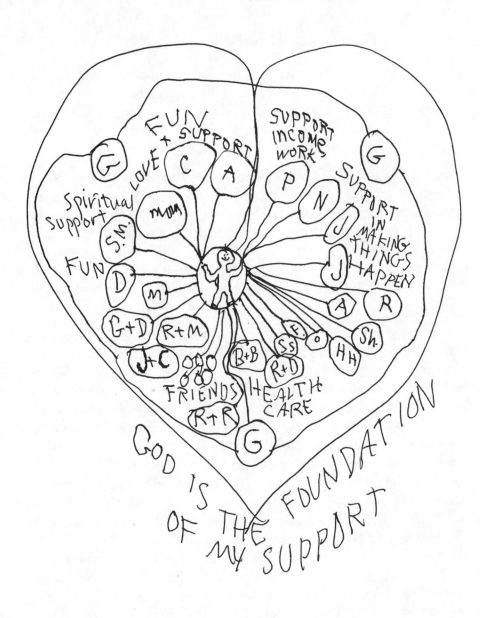

THE POWER OF SUPPORT GROUPS

There is something immensely empowering about coming out of isolation and sharing our private struggles with others who have walked the same path. Lending an open ear and an open heart, and embracing our common humanity, is an ennobling experience. It is a gift we give both to ourselves and to others.

Whether the focus is fighting cancer, recovering from drug abuse, or achieving success in business, the power of a peer support group can have a major impact on one's life. We have seen this documented in numerous grass-roots movements. The personal-growth and consciousness-raising groups of the seventies formed the foundation of the women's movement. The most popular support groups of the eighties were the ones that dealt with addictions, life-threatening illness, and career success.

I have led many ongoing support groups as an art therapist and career consultant, and have seen amazing results. Groups in which members state their personal goals, discuss internal and external obstacles, and receive support and resources from the group, are particularly effective. For instance, Penny was a member of one of my journal classes focusing on job satisfaction and career choice. Penny was looking for a counseling job and began describing the kind of environment she wanted to work in: white walls, lots of windows and light, lush green plants everywhere. I suggested she draw a picture of her "dream job" with an emphasis on the physical environment, since that seemed so important to her. Within three days she called me and said that she would have to drop out of the group, which met during the day, because she had found a job. Penny told me that upon walking into the office for the interview, she knew she had found *her* work environment—large windows, plants hanging everywhere, and a light, airy atmosphere. The interior was just as she had described it to our group and portrayed it in her picture. As it turned out, she was hired on the spot. Later Penny told me that she was so happy being in that particular setting that the quality of her counseling work improved dramatically.

I have also seen the immense value of support teams in my corporate work: increased morale, better communication, improved performance, and greater job satisfaction. This leads to career advancement that means far greater fulfillment for the individual employee as well as long-term benefits to the company. I often do problem solving through drawing or visual thinking on paper in these corporate groups. The opening up of creative right-brain functions which occurs as a result of these techniques carries over into work tasks. These graphic brainstorming techniques are especially effective for people who work in creative divisions or research/development groups within corporations.

HOW TO CREATE A SUPPORT GROUP

You can start your own support group by inviting two or more people to join you in mutual support. You do not need prior experience or training in group leadership, because you can suggest revolving "leadership": each session will be facilitated by a different member. The ground rules are as follows:

1. *Members make a commitment to attend the group for a minimum of four weeks and recommit to membership on a monthly basis.* There are no "drop-ins," no visitors, and no observers. Everyone is required to participate.

2. Each session is a minimum of two hours long. A longer period may be needed if the group is large (more than eight). Twelve is about maximum size for allowing participation of all members.

3. *Members set their own goals and state them clearly for the group.* For example:

   "I want to start my own business."

   "I want to get my master's degree and become a counselor."

   "I want to write a book."

   "I want a long-term, committed love relationship."

   "I want to buy a home."

   "I want to heal myself from chronic headaches."

"I want a part-time job that pays enough to support 'time off' for my personal needs: classes, travel, hobbies, and friends."

"I want to get clear on my goals and priorities in life."

4. *Members discuss the obstacles to achieving their goals.* Some of these barriers are internal and attitudinal (low self-esteem, fear of failure, lack of confidence); other barriers are external or technical (lack of training or credentials, inadequate information, lack of local resources). The group energy is very important in helping members deal with obstacles. The perspective and experience of others can help us expand our horizons and come away with good ideas we have never considered before. Also, the potential for networking to resources and people is greatly increased.

5. *No criticism is allowed.* A support team must be a safe place to explore one's innermost dreams for personal fulfillment. It is a place to brainstorm and then to ground one's wildest imaginings in day-to-day reality. Such creative visioning and follow-through do not thrive in an atmosphere of ridicule, judgment, or criticism.

6. *Leadership of a grass-roots support group is democratic.* A new facilitator is selected for each weekly session. This prevents any one member from dominating the group with his or her own agenda or point of view. The goal is for everybody to participate fully and to claim "ownership" in the group. This approach to leadership has been successfully used for over fifty years in Twelve-Step programs.

7. *No cross-talk or interruptions are allowed while an individual is presenting his or her goals, current obstacles, and successes.* It is essential that members be free to fully express their own personal process. After sharing an update, the individual who has the floor is then free to invite feedback and resource sharing.

8. *In order to create a safe and trusting environment, confidentiality is advised.* Trust provides a solid group foundation. Confidentiality allows everyone to be themselves and to fully express their hopes, dreams, and fears, without the risk of being misunderstood or judged by outsiders.

9. *Successes are celebrated.* Each time a member achieves a significant goal (as self-defined), he or she reports it to the group for a communal celebration. The individual can be honored with a bouquet of flowers, a toast, a potluck dinner, or a special group outing. It is important to acknowledge our own growth and share that special moment with others.

10. A *buddy system, which carries over into everyday life, is encouraged among group members.* There is something special about knowing that you will be able to receive help in times of need—getting a ride, finding a baby-sitter, having someone to talk to. Maybe you had a best friend in childhood—someone you could talk to about anything—someone you could always count on. A support-group buddy can be that kind of a pal. Many lasting friendships have begun in support groups. Long after the group has disbanded, and members have moved away, some individuals have stayed in touch for years and continue to share their dreams and successes.

I was part of a women's support group for two and a half years. These were challenging times for all the women in the group. Each one of us was embarking on major life changes: healing relationships, getting divorces, changing careers, starting new business ventures, returning to school, and healing chronic illnesses. The results of the weekly group support were phenomenal.

At a reunion two years after the group disbanded, we celebrated each woman's triumph. Pamela was now living in a Malibu condominium, which she had visualized and drawn in her journal, and was operating a successful children's art school in her studio. Gabriele had earned both her B.A. and M.A. degrees and was now in private practice as a counselor. Maureen had gotten a divorce and started a new job and a new life. Nancy V. had developed a toy product and received a patent, and was now presenting it to potential manufacturers. Rhoda, who had returned to school to receive training in psychology, had become a marriage, family, and child counselor and was conducting groups for women. Kathleen was now marketing children's story-telling tapes which she had written, narrated, and produced. Nancy S. made a successful career change into writing and publishing, and manifested a loving, nurturing relationship that later led to a happy marriage. As for myself, I had fully recovered from a very difficult divorce, expanded my work to include corporate consulting, and completed my second manuscript for a book that was later published. In the end, each one of us attained her heart's desire.

RAINBOW HEART MEDITATION

Purpose: Creating your own personal support system; expressing gratitude to those who support you; experiencing yourself being loved and supported.

Materials: Paper and colored felt pens.

Imagine that you are standing in a large circle of people, holding hands. The individuals in this circle are members of your personal support system. As you look around the circle, notice who they are. See each one of them clearly, and notice the expressions of love and support on their faces. They may be family members, friends, loved ones, pets, neighbors, coworkers, and supportive professionals.

Imagine that there is a laser beam of white light emanating from your heart and from the hearts of all the people in the circle. These beams of heart light come together in the center of the circle to form a pool of healing energy. From this pool of light a fountain of rainbows rises high into the sky. As the rainbows arc back down to earth, each one enters the crown of a person in the circle, filling him or her with rainbow light.

Now, meditate on the qualities of the seven colors of the rainbow. First is the color red, blazing with courage, strength, and passion for life. Second is the color orange, which glows with enthusiasm, vitality, and joy. Third is the color yellow, bringing clarity and insight. With green, the fourth color of the spectrum, comes balance and abundance. Fifth is the color blue, which infuses peace and harmony. The sixth ray is indigo (deep violet-blue), bringing inner knowledge and wisdom. The seventh and final ray is violet, which helps you contact your Inner Power or spirit within. White light, which contains all the colors of the rainbow, brings spiritual regeneration.

Now, in any way you choose, draw a picture of yourself expressing gratitude to the members of your support circle. You might show yourself giving gifts to each one of them.

Draw a picture of your Rainbow Heart Meditation. Let it be as free and fanciful as you wish. What would your ideal support group look like? (It does not have to be a formal group but can be an informal circle of friends.)

Now draw yourself showing how you feel being surrounded by loving, accepting people in your life.

Postscript

Now that you have become familiar with the philosophy and methods presented in this book, let me make a few suggestions.

If you have read the book without doing the exercises, that is fine. Hopefully you have gained a greater understanding of what this approach is all about. Now, I urge you to go back to Chapter 1 and begin again. This time, *do the exercises*! Experience the message of the book firsthand by using the exercises in the order in which they are given. There is no substitute for *your own experience*. And my work is, above all, experiential. It simply cannot be fully grasped through reading about it or looking at the pictures. If it seems like a method that suits you, try it. That will be the only way to find out if it works for you.

On the other hand, you may have already done some or all of the exercises. If so, be aware that this is an ongoing process. You can do these exercises over and over again, and still benefit from them. I have been using them successfully for many years and so have hundreds of my students and clients. You might be wondering: "Well, if these methods work, why do you have to keep doing them?" Because healing and wholeness are a never-ending process. New issues and challenges present themselves on a daily basis. That's life.

In continuing to use these techniques, you do not have to follow the linear sequence again. When you have become familiar with the exercises, choose the one that is relevant to your particular needs. For instance, one day you may be dealing with physical pain, so you would use the exercises in chapter 4. Another day, you may want to do some broad-scale life and career planning with the material in chapters 7 and 8. At still another time, you may need to vent strong feelings or frustrations by doing the exercises in chapter 2. I trust that you will find the technique that is most appropriate for you at any given time.

You have in your hands a collection of powerful tools for turning crises into opportunities and problems into gifts. As you transform the raw materials of life's experiences into precious gems of insight and wisdom, your Inner Artist will emerge. And it is through embracing this Inner Artist that the secrets of healing will be revealed to you. Love, the divine power that can heal your life, resides in your very own heart. It has always been there, waiting only to be liberated.

Bibliography

Achterberg, Jean. *Imagery in Healing: Shamanism and Modern Medicine.* Boston: Shambhala, 1985.

Benson, Herbert, M.D. *The Relaxation Response.* New York: Avon Books, 1976.

Borysenko, Joan, Ph.D. *Minding the Body, Mending the Mind.* New York: Bantam Books, 1988.

Campbell, Joseph, with Bill Moyers. *The Power of Myth.* New York: Doubleday, 1988.

Capacchione, Lucia. *The Power of Your Other Hand.* North Hollywood: Newcastle, 1988.

_____. *The Creative Journal.* North Hollywood: Newcastle, 1989.

_____. *The Well-Being Journal.* North Hollywood: Newcastle, 1989.

Capacchione, Lucia, with Elizabeth Johnson and James Strohecker. *Lighten Up Your Body, Lighten Up Your Life.* North Hollywood: Newcastle, 1990.

Chia, Mantak. *Taoist Ways to Transform Stress into Vitality.* Huntington, New York: Healing Tao Books, 1985.

_____. *Chi Self-Massage: The Taoist Way of Rejuvenation.* Huntington: Healing Tao Books, 1986.

Chopra, Deepak, M.D. *Creating Health: Beyond Prevention, Toward Perfection.* Boston: Houghton Mifflin, 1987.

_____. *Quantum Healing: Exploring the Frontiers of Mind/Body Medicine.* New York: Bantam Books, 1989.

Cousins, Norman. *Anatomy of an Illness.* New York: W.W. Norton, 1979.

_____. *The Healing Heart.* New York: Avon Books, 1983.

Dychtwald, Ken. *Bodymind.* New York: Jove Publications, 1978.

Gawain, Shakti. *Creative Visualization.* New York: Bantam Books, 1979.

_____. *Living in the Light.* Berkeley: Whatever Publishing, 1986.

Gendlin, Eugene. *Focusing.* New York: Bantam Books, 1982.

Hay, Louise L. *You Can Heal Your Life*. Santa Monica, California: Hay House, 1987.

_____. *Heal Your Body*. Santa Monica, California: Hay House, 1982.

_____. *I Love My Body*. Santa Monica, California: Hay House, 1987.

_____. *The AIDS Book: Creating a Positive Approach*. Santa Monica, California: Hay House, 1988.

Jaffe, Dennis T. *Healing From Within*. New York: Alfred A. Knopf, 1980.

Jampolsky, Gerald, M.D. *Love Is Letting Go of Fear*. Berkeley: Celestial Arts, 1979.

_____. *There Is a Rainbow Behind Every Dark Cloud*. Berkeley: Celestial Arts, 1978.

Johnson, Robert. *Inner Work: Using Dreams and Active Imagination for Personal Growth*. New York: Harper & Row, 1987.

Joy, Brugh, M.D. *Joy's Way*. Los Angeles: Jeremy P. Tarcher, 1978.

Kurtz, Ron, and Hector Prestera. *The Body Reveals*. New York: Harper & Row, 1976.

La Berge, Stephen. *Lucid Dreaming: The Power of Being Aware in Your Dreams*. New York: Ballantine, 1986.

Lad, Vasant. *Ayurveda: The Science of Self-Healing*. Santa Fe: Lotus Press, 1984.

Locke, Stephen, and Douglas Colligan. *The Healer Within*. New York: E.P. Dutton, 1986.

Mindell, Arnold. *Working with the Dreaming Body*. Boston: Routledge & Kegan Paul, 1985.

Muramoto, Naboru. *Healing Ourselves*. New York: Avon Books, 1973.

Ornstein, Robert, and David Sobel. *The Healing Brain: Breakthrough Discoveries About How the Brain Keeps Us Healthy*. New York: Simon & Schuster, 1987.

Oyle, Irving. *The Healing Mind*. Berkeley: Celestial Arts, 1979.

_____. *The New American Medicine Show/Discovering the Healing Connection*. Berkeley: Celestial Arts, 1979.

Pelletier, Kenneth R. *Mind as Healer, Mind as Slayer*. New York: Dell, 1977.

Prudden, Suzy. *MetaFitness*. Santa Monica, California: Hay House, 1989.

Rossman, Martin, M.D. *Healing Yourself: A Step-by-Step Program for Better Health through Imagery*. New York: Walker & Co., 1987.

Sanford, John A. *Healing and Wholeness*. New York: Paulist Press, 1977.

Segal, Jeanne. *Living Beyond Fear: A Course for Coping with the Emotional Aspects of Life-Threatening Illnesses.* North Hollywood: Newcastle, 1984.

Selye, Hans, M.D. *The Stress of Life.* New York: McGraw-Hill, 1978.

Shealy, Norman O., M.D., and Caroline Myss. *The Creation of Health.* Walpole, New Hampshire: Stillpoint, 1989.

Shorr, Joseph E. *Go See the Movie in Your Head.* New York: Popular Library, 1977.

Siegel, Bernard, M.D. *Love, Medicine & Miracles.* New York: Harper & Row, 1986.

———. *Peace, Love & Healing.* New York: Harper & Row, 1989.

Simonton, O. Carl, M.D., Stephanie Matthews-Simonton, and James L. Creighton. *Getting Well Again.* New York: Bantam Books, 1978.

Stone, Christopher. *Re-Creating Your Self.* Portland: Metamorphous Press, 1988.

Stone, Hal, and Sidra Winkelman. *Embracing Our Selves.* San Rafael: New World Library, 1989.

———. *Embracing Each Other.* San Rafael: New World Library, 1989.

Strozzi-Heckler, Richard, Ph.D. *Anatomy of Change: Awakening the Wisdom of the Body.* Boston: Shambhala, 1984.

Vaughn, Frances. *Awakening Intuition.* New York: Doubleday, 1979.